D1252595

Délices de France

Fish & Seafood

Délices de France

Fish & Seafood

DINE WITH FRANCE'S MASTER CHEFS

KÖNEMANN

Acknowledgements

We would like to thank the following people and businesses for their valuable contributions to this project:

Baccarat, Paris; Champagne Veuve Clicquot Ponsardin, Reims; Cristallerie de Hartzviller, Hartzviller; Cristallerie Haute-Bretagne, Paris; Établissements Depincé Laiteries Mont-Saint-Michel, Saint-Brice; FCR Porcelaine Daniel Hechter, Paris; Harraca/Roehl Design, Paris; La Verrerie Durobor, Soigny (Belgien); Le Creuset Fonte Émaillée, Fresnoy-le-Grand; Renoleau, Angoulême; Maison Mossler Orfèvre Fabricant, Paris; Manridal, Wasselonne; Moulinex, Bagnolet; Pavillon Christofle, Paris; Porcelaine Lafarge-Limoges, Limoges; Porcelaines Bernardaud, Limoges; Porcelaines de Sologne et Créations Cacharel, Lamotte-Beuvron; Porcelaines Raynaud, Limoges; Rémy & Associés Distribution France, Levallois-Perret; Robert Havilland et C. Parlon, Paris; SCOF, St-Rémy-sur-Durolle; Tupperware, Rueil-Malmaison; Villeroy & Boch, Garges-lès-Gonesse; Zanussi CLV Système, Torcy.

Level of difficulty of the recipes:

★ easy

★★ advanced

★★★ challenging

Original title: Délices de France, Poissons, Crustacés
Photographs: Michel Tessier
Wine recommendations: Georges Ciret
(Member of the Association of Professional Sommeliers)

Translation from French: Tim Jones
English-language editor: John Elian
Coordination and typesetting: Agents – Producers – Editors, Overath
Reproduction: Reproservice Werner Pees
Production manager: Detlev Schaper
Printing and binding: Leefung Asco Printers, Hong Kong

Printed in China

ISBN 3-8290-2745-1

10 9 8 7 6 5 4 3 2 1

Contents

Foreword

Dining culture is an art that draws people together and fosters harmony. A nation's cuisine is without doubt one of the most important values of any developed civilization, and familiarity with "foreign food" contributes—perhaps even more than we realize—to increased tolerance and mutual understanding between different cultures.

The sixteenth-century French poet Rabelais was well aware of this as he wrote in Pantagruel, "Every rational human being who builds a house starts with the kitchen...." And before setting off for the Congress of Vienna in 1815, the French foreign minister Talleyrand reminded his king, Louis XVIII, "Sire, I need pots far more than instructions...." For these reasons, I am delighted with the publication of this unique collections of recipes.

This is a comprehensive work; it gathers together many of the best chefs working in France today, representing different regions and professional organizations as well as outstanding masters from the various branches of the French dining tradition that have made the culinary culture of this nation so famous. All the contributors have already made a name for themselves, or are well on their way to doing so. This work, therefore, with its wealth of practical details and background information, will appeal to anyone with culinary interests—from the hobby cook looking to impress guests at a dinner party to the experienced gourmet interested in improving their craft.

Roger Roucou
President of the *Maîtres Cuisiniers de France*, 1988

Chefs' Foreword

For perhaps the first time in history, the recipes of a large number of well-known chefs are gathered together in a comprehensive collection of the delicacies of French cuisine. French cooking is revered throughout the world, and we believe that we can be proud of this portion of our cultural heritage, which so greatly enhances the pleasures of life.

This cookbook offers a broad panorama of carefully selected culinary delights and seeks to build a bridge between experts from the various gastronomic professions and all friends of fine dining. It gives us, the chefs, the possibility to set down our expertise n writing and to disseminate our professional secrets, thus enriching and furthering the Art of Cooking. Once a luxury, haute cuisine is no longer limited to the patrons of elegant restaurants. The recipes presented here range in difficulty from straightforward to quite complex, and are intended to offer you ideas and encouragement in the preparation of your daily meals.

Allow yourself to be inspired! In this collection you will find novelties, acquaint yourself with regional and exotic specialties, and rediscover old favorites. There is a strong continuity between these recipes and the great tradition of French cooking—a rich and varied table offering a broad palette of gourmet pleasures ranging from the simple and light to the extravagant. We have dedicated our lives to this cuisine and are delighted to invite you on this voyage of culinary exploration.

We have made the details in the recipes as clear as possible in order to make it easier to try them at home. In this process, we illustrate our art, which provides a treat both for the palate and for the eye—two pleasures that go hand-in-hand in cooking. With a little practice, you will soon be skilled enough to turn the everyday into the extraordinary, and to impress your guests with culinary masterpieces.

In a special way, the art of cooking fosters the social, interpersonal side of life: It is no coincidence that food accompanies all the important milestones of our lives, from a family sitting down together at the table to holiday celebrations and weddings to business deals and political meetings.

We are pleased to present you with our most successful creations, so that you can share their pleasures with your loved ones. And we hope that you will have as much fun trying out these recipes as we did creating them.

Furthermore, we hope that the culinary specialties presented here may serve as an ambassador throughout the world for the enjoyment and pleasures of life, and that this book may contribute both to mutual understanding among cultures and to the refinement of culinary delights.

Good luck in trying out the recipes!
From the chefs of *Délices de France*

Lemon Sole

1. Peel and finely chop the shallots.

Ingredients:
4 lemon soles
3 shallots
2 cups/500 ml beer
2 cups/500 ml
crème fraîche
6½ tbsp/100 g butter
1 bunch of chervil
salt and pepper

Serves 4
Preparation time: 20 minutes
Cooking time: 30 minutes
Difficulty: ★

2. Thoroughly clean the lemon soles. Trim the fins and tail using scissors, then scale the fish very carefully. Grease the baking dish and sprinkle in the chopped shallots.

The lemon sole inhabits northern waters, no further south than the Bay of Biscay. The lean flesh of this flatfish is delicate in flavor as well as rich in potassium.
Since lemon soles lose significant volume during cooking, it is best to choose large ones. You can have the soles trimmed at the time of purchase if you wish; the brown skin is removed after the soles have been cooked. It is better to use pale fish since darker sole is often too strong.
The beer should cover the fish only up to its spine, not all the way, and should be simmered rather than boiled. Cover the skin with buttered paper to prevent it from turning crisp; if it does, the flesh may be torn when removing it.
The cooking juices, crème fraîche and butter are all you will require for the sauce—no need to prepare another sauce that could only take longer and be less tasty. After adding the butter, heat the sauce just long enough to melt the butter, and not so long that the sauce boils and clarifies.
This dish, with all its Nordic blondness, should be served very hot, perhaps with boiled potatoes or poached vegetables. It cannot be reheated.
Our wine expert feels that the iodized characteristics of a coastal wine like a Muscadet sur lie will go splendidly with these flatfish.

3. Place the fish in the pan. Season with salt and pepper.

4. Pour the beer over the fish and cook in a hot oven for about 20 minutes.

in Beer Sauce

5. Take the fish out of the pan and remove the brown skin. Place them on a serving platter. Reduce the remaining liquid to ¾ of its original volume, add the crème fraîche, and let the sauce thicken.

6. Strain the sauce through a fine sieve into a saucepan. Whisk in butter and heat to just shy of boiling. Serve the fish with the beer sauce and garnish with a few sprigs of chervil.

Fish

1. *Peel the shallots, carrots and turnips. Finely chop the shallots and cut the turnip and carrots into pear-shaped pieces. Halve and seed the zucchini, then cut them into pear-shaped pieces as well.*

Ingredients:
7 oz/200 g burbot fillets
7 oz/200 g salmon fillets
7 oz/200 g sole fillets
7 oz/200 g turbot fillets
4 langoustines
1¾ oz/50 g shallots
4 carrots
4 turnips
3 zucchini
1 small green cabbage
13 tbsp/200 g butter
6½ tbsp/100 ml white wine
salt and pepper

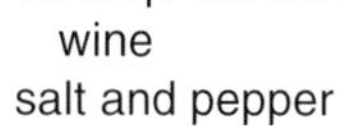

Serves 4
Preparation time: 45 minutes
Cooking time: 50 minutes
Difficulty ★

2. *Bone all the fish (burbot, salmon, sole, turbot) and scallop the fillets of each into 4 thin slices.*

As the name suggests, this pot-au-feu is a little out of the ordinary, featuring a variety of fish rather than meat. While the choice of fish has more to do with aesthetic considerations of color than with any gastronomic necessity, it is essential to use fish that require the same cooking time, and whose fillets will stay intact without desintegrating. To prevent this, they should be cooked gently without boiling, which will also prevent film from forming.

The wine should not cover the fillets completely—half-covered is enough—and the vegetables should stay crisp. Let the sauce reduce well to minimize the acidity of the white wine, then add butter and boil it again for a while to keep it from souring.

Serve this delicious dish to any fans of sea-food stews, or to delight and warm the hearts of the entire household.

The advice of our wine expert: The refreshing, lively nature of a Chablis will harmonize the saltiness of the fish with the sweetness of the vegetables.

3. *Simmer the carrots, turnips and zucchini in separate pots of lightly salted water. When they are just tender, cool and set aside.*

4. *Shred the cabbage and brown it in a saucepan with 3½ tbsp/50 g of the butter. Salt lightly, add pepper, cover and cook for 20 minutes.*

Pot-Au-Feu

5. Cover the bottom of a greased baking dish with the chopped shallots. Place slices of salmon, sole, burbot and turbot—4 rows of 4 slices each—in the dish. Season with salt and pepper. Add ¾ cup/200 ml water and the white wine and simmer. Remove the fish, add the langoustines to the liquid and simmer.

6. Strain the liquid through a fine sieve and reduce to ¾ of its original volume, then whip in the remaining butter. Place the shredded cabbage in a pile on the serving platter and arrange the slices of fish and the vegetables around it. Add the langoustines, pour on the sauce and serve very hot.

Sole Soufflée

1. *Remove the skin from each sole. Cut back the flesh along three quarters of the backbone, forming a flap on each side as shown, then slide a knife under the backbone to remove it.*

Ingredients:
4 soles
16 slices soft white bread
4 shallots
8 cloves garlic
7 oz/200 g parsley, finely chopped
2 egg whites
4 tbsp crème fraîche
6½ tbsp/100 ml oil
juice of 4 lemons
13 tbsp/200 g butter
salt and pepper

Serves 4
Preparation time: 1 hour
Cooking time: 15 minutes
Difficulty: ★ ★

The sole, with its perfectly oval shape, has long been prized by epicures; even the Romans were extremely fond of it. Removing the backbone requires quite a bit of practice, so if you doubt you are up to the task, have it done at the time of purchase, making sure they are cut on the black side. Soles are always served lying on their bellies. Flour the undersides of the soles thoroughly so that they do not stick to the frying-pan during cooking. Covering the pan with foil allows the fish to steam on the stovetop, or they can be baked in the oven.
Make sure the soles do not turn too brown. To check how far a fillet is cooked, simply lift it; if it comes away easily, the fish is done.
The butter sauce should be served frothy and, like Sole Soufflé "Hermitage" itself, as soon as it is ready.
Serve this regal dish as a light, elegant meal; its delicacy is impressive.
Our wine expert feels that the delicate flavor of sole merits a very fine white Burgundy and recommends a Meursault Charmes.

2. *Remove the crusts from the bread, then crumble the bread in a food processor.*

3. *Peel the shallots and garlic, and finely chop them and the parsley. Mix first the chopped shallots and parsley, then the garlic,*

4. *Pour the egg whites and the crème fraîche into the mixture. Add salt and pepper and stir vigorously to obtain a smooth paste.*

“Hermitage”

5. Open up the soles. Stuff each with 2 tbsp of the bread crumb mixture. The soles will appear rounded. Fold the flaps back over the stuffing.

6. Add salt and pepper, then fry the soles in the oil without turning them. Finish cooking them either by steaming or baking them (see above). When they are done, skim the oil off the juices in the pan, add the lemon juice and whisk in the butter. Serve the fish with this sauce.

Angler Fish

1. Peel and chop the garlic. Mince the carrot, onion, leek and white beet leaves. Finely chop the parsley.

Ingredients:
3 lb 5 oz/1.5 kg angler fish
2 cloves garlic
1 carrot
1 onion
1 leek
2 white beet leaves
parsley
1 tbsp oil
2 tbsp tomato concentrate
6½ tbsp/100 ml Noilly Prat vermouth
1 cup/250 ml mayonnaise (see basic recipe)
1 baguette
garlic
salt and pepper

Serves 6
Preparation time: 20 minutes
Cooking time: 20 minutes
Difficulty ★

Agathoise sauce, which has a rich cultural tradition in France, is a miracle of flavor. Angler fish—also known as monkfish or sea devil—tastes particularly good with it, though spotted dogfish, turbot or the John Dory are also delicious with agathoise sauce. This recipe can be your inspiration to further explore its possibilities with other dishes. Our chef offers these suggestions: The mayonnaise should not be overcooked or it will turn, and the angler fish should be cooked, uncovered, over high heat.
Boiled potatoes and creole rice make fine side dishes for this entrée. Such a feast is sure to be eaten up entirely, which is fortunate, since Angler Fish with Agathoise Sauce cannot be reheated.
To complement the Mediterranean sunlight this dish brings to your table, our wine suggestion is a Bandol Blanc de Blanc, a white wine full of fruit.

2. Bone the angler fish and cut it into cubes about 1½ in/3-4 cm across. Place these in a saucepan. Add the tomato concentrate, vermouth, and salt and pepper.

3. Mix in the beet leaves, onion and leeks.

4. Add the parsley and garlic, and stir into the mixture. Cook for about 15 minutes over low heat.

with Agathoise Sauce

5. When it is done, place the angler fish on a serving platter. Pour the mayonnaise into a separate saucepan.

6. Bring the liquid in which the fish was cooked to a boil, then pour it into the mayonnaise while beating vigorously. Keep the heat low, and do not let it boil. Coat the angler fish with this agathoise sauce and serve with slices of baguette rubbed with garlic.

Stuffed

1. *Peel and finely chop the onion and 2 shallots, and mince the chervil and tarragon. Fry half of each of the chopped ingredients in a saucepan with the olive oil. Clean and dice the mushrooms.*

2. *Scale, trim and gut the hogfish, setting aside the liver. Chop the liver. Add half the mushrooms and the chopped liver to the sautéed mixture. Season with salt and pepper and cook over low heat.*

Ingredients:
1 2 lb 3-oz/1-kg hogfish
1 onion
3 shallots
½ bunch chervil
1 sprig tarragon
3½ oz/100 g mushrooms
1 tsp olive oil
1 small glass of milk
4 tomatoes
½ cup/120 ml dry white wine
1 cup/250 ml fish stock (see basic recipe)
6½ tbsp/100 ml heavy cream
salt and pepper

Serves 4
Preparation time: 35 minutes
Cooking time: 45 minutes
Difficulty ✯

The hogfish, a reddish rockfish with coppery tones, is firm of flesh. This striking denizen of the Mediterranean only rears its fossil-like head at the market in spring and summer, so keep an eye out for it with this dish in mind. However, the gilthead or the sea bass can be effective substitutes for this delicious, venerable fish from the the ocean's depths.

While this recipe is not difficult, it is important to take care when cooking the fish; it needs more time than ordinary, more tender fish. The hogfish's gelatinous texture renders it ideal for thickening sauces.

When adding the heavy cream to the sauce, do so over low heat. The sauce is ready when it coats the spoon. Serve hot with rice pilaf, a worthy accompaniment.

If you have yet to discover the delights of hogfish liver, this recipe will make you an aficionado. Rarely served except in southern France, Stuffed Hogfish will enchant all your guests with its novelty.

The wonderful, discreet fruitiness of a fine Chablis cannot be excelled here, according to our wine expert. From the seven *grands crus* available, choose a "Le Clos" if possible, the most mellow in taste.

3. *Place the rest of the mushrooms, shallots, onions, chervil and tarragon in another saucepan. Pour in the milk, salt lightly, add pepper and cook over low heat.*

4. *Stuff the hogfish with the sautéed mixture. Seed, chop and crush the tomatoes. Peel and finely chop the remaining shallot.*

Hogfish

5. Place the hogfish in an ovenproof dish and sprinkle the chopped shallot over it. Pour in the white wine and fish stock. Add salt and pepper, and bake for about 20 minutes in a hot oven. When finished, strain the cooking liquid into a saucepan.

6. Reduce the cooking juices by half. Blend the milk mixture in a food processor and add to the reduced stock along with the tomatoes and cream, and let the mixture thicken over low heat. Remove the skin from the hogfish, and cover the fish with sauce. Serve hot sprinkled with minced chervil.

Bream with

1. Slice the zucchini very thin, then grill the peppers for a few minutes either in a very hot oven or over a gas flame.

Ingredients:
- 4 bream fillets, each weighing 6 oz/180 g
- 3½ oz/100 g small zucchini
- 5¼ oz/150 g sweet red peppers
- 13 tbsp/200 g butter
- salt and pepper

Serves 4
Preparation time: 20 minutes
Cooking time: 25 minutes
Difficulty: ★

2. Peel the peppers, remove their seeds, then thoroughly purée the flesh in a food processor. Cook the sauce thus obtained over low heat. Season with salt and pepper.

Culinary innovation or artful metamorphosis—either phrase could describe how a sea fish comes to be decorated with tasty green zucchini scales. This simple, quick recipe, a delight to prepare, combines vivid color with full flavor and results in a meal most epicures will savor.
Either sea bass or John Dory would make a fine substitute for the bream.
To obtain smooth consistency in the butter and red pepper sauce, cook the peppers just until the moment you can easily remove their skins.
Serve this dish very hot with artichoke hearts as a side dish. It does not keep and cannot be reheated.
Our wine expert suggests that, as a fine dish merits a fine wine, you should fetch a Meursault Charmes from your cellar.

3. Strain the sauce through a fine sieve and simmer for 1 minute over low heat. Adjust the seasoning if necessary.

4. Add half of the butter to the sauce; do not allow it to boil. Set the sauce aside in a double boiler.

Zucchini Scales

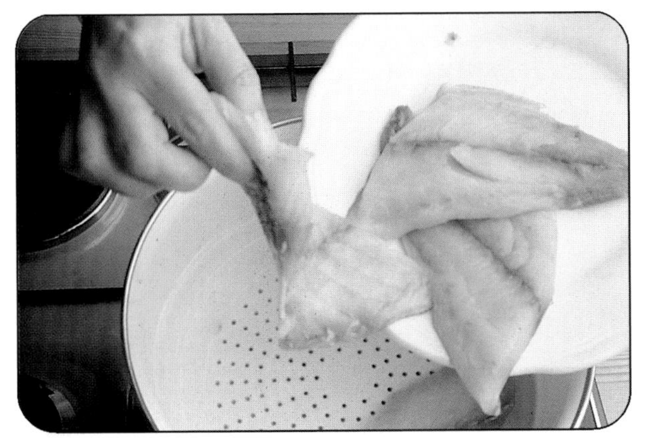

5. Sprinkle a little salt and pepper on the bream slices and steam them for a few minutes.

6. Briefly sauté the zucchini slices in some of the butter, then arrange them like scales on the bream. Melt the remaining butter and pour it on the fish, then place the fillets on a serving platter with the pepper sauce.

Glazed Salmon

1. *Seed and dice the tomatoes. Trim the asparagus, poach the tips briefly in a little boiling water, then cut them in quarters. Finely chop the mushrooms.*

Ingredients:
4 scallops of fresh salmon
2 tomatoes
1 lb 5 oz/600 g green asparagus
3½ oz/100 g *trompette de la morte* mushrooms
1 bunch chives
6½ tbsp/100 ml lobster bisque (see basic recipe)
6½ tbsp/100 ml heavy cream
salt

Serves 4
Preparation time: 15 minutes
Cooking time: 20 minutes
Difficulty: ★

2. *Cut the chives into short sticks and set aside.*

While asparagus was actually cultivated in France as early as the 17th century, it was only at the end of the 19th century that it became a specialty of the area around Orléans. This was thanks to a gendarme who collected some samples near Argenteuil during the siege of Paris and totally devoted himself to cultivating them after his discharge.
Our chef recommends wild asparagus, which has more character than its cultivated cousin; its strong personality will mark this dish. Depending on the season, salmon trout or landlocked salmon may substitute for wild salmon.
Quick and simple, Glazed Salmon with Asparagus should be served hot, immediately after cooking. It will not keep. Any meal, festive or intimate, will be enhanced by the flavors of this dish.
Our wine expert suggests a Pouilly-Fumé, because the Sauvignon grape is, in his opinion, ideal with salmon in any form.

3. *Bone the salmon scallops, then salt and steam them.*

4. *Reheat the lobster bisque and add the mushrooms to it. Simmer briefly.*

with Asparagus

5. Cover the salmon scallops with the chives, chopped tomatoes and asparagus tips.

6. Whip the cream and gently stir it into the bisque. Arrange the fish on a serving platter and cover them with the sauce. Place the platter under a broiler briefly to glaze. Serve very hot.

Roast Bream

1. Peel the garlic cloves, then blanch them in 4-5 changes of unsalted water. Cut the cloves in half, discard the green stem, and purée in a food processor.

Ingredients:
4 bream filets, 6⅓ oz/ 180 g each
6 cloves of garlic
7 oz/200 g tomatoes
2 lemons
1 bulb of fennel
2 lb 3 oz/1 kg zucchini
1¾ oz/50 g shallots
1 tsp/4 g saffron
6½ tbsp/100 ml white wine
¾ cup/200 ml fish stock (see basic recipe)
6½ tbsp/100 ml cream
¼ cup/60 g butter
1 tbsp/10 g dried *trompette de la mort* mushrooms, ground
salt and pepper

Serves 4
Preparation time: 40 minutes
Cooking time: 30 minutes
Difficulty: ★

2. Peel 3 of the tomatoes and the lemons and cut the fruits into thin rounds. Bone the bream fillets.

Saffron, originally from the Orient, was brought to Spain by the Arabs and has been cultivated in France since the 16th century. The spice is made from the stigmas of a small, purple crocus, which are dried either as brown threads or a yellow powder with a bitter taste and a pungent aroma. Well-known in ancient times and the Middle Ages, it was used not only for cooking but also in making medicines and dye.

It fell briefly out of favor for a time, only being used, as Alexandre Dumas noted, "to give color to cakes, vermicelli and butter," before making a vigorous comeback in diverse regional cuisines.

Make this dish in the summertime, when zucchini and fresh fennel are at their finest. Sea bass or hogfish fillets may substitute for the bream.

Roast Bream Supreme with Saffron should be served very hot—it will not keep. Other than the time it takes to prepare the vegetables, this recipe will not present any difficulties. This subtly original dish is a veritable potpourri of mingled flavors that makes for a memorable dinner.

Our wine expert advises using this opportunity to discover for yourself the very particular aroma of a Riesling.

3. Cut up the fennel and arrange it in the bottom of a baking dish. Salt and pepper the bream fillets. Place them on top of the fennel pieces and coat them with the garlic purée.

4. Arrange the tomato and lemon rounds attractively on top of the fish fillets.

Supreme with Saffron

5. Bake the bream fillets in a hot oven for 10 minutes. Cut the zucchini into spaghetti-like strips and cook them briefly in lightly salted boiling water. Peel and finely chop the shallots and remaining tomato.

6. Sauté the shallots in a little butter. Add the saffron, white wine and fish stock, reduce until most of the liquid has evaporated, then mix in the cream. Whip in the butter and heat. Cover a serving platter with the sauce and arrange the fish fillets on it. Serve with the steamed zucchini strips and ground mushrooms.

Fisherman's Bourride

1. Scale the fish. Bone the monkfish and cut it into pieces. Remove the eyes and rinse the heads and bones in fresh water. Slice 1 of the onions and mince the shallots.

Ingredients:

3 lb 6½ oz/1.6 kg white fish: 2 with firm flesh (monk-fish or conger eel) and 2 with tender flesh (sea bass, whiting or John Dory)
2 medium-sized onions
1 shallot
1 cup/250 ml olive oil
dried sprigs of fennel
bay leaves, coriander and thyme
6 cloves garlic
5 egg yolks
1 cup/250 ml peanut oil
1 lb 3 oz/600 g potatoes
2 cups/500 ml fish stock (see basic recipe)
1 baguette

Serves 6
Preparation time: 40 minutes
Cooking time: 30 minutes
Difficulty: ☆ ☆

This dish, which originally comes from Säte, is redolent of the sea. More than just a fish soup, bourride is a meal in and of itself. The one described here is the true bourride of Provence in its purest, most authentic form. These days, some restaurants serve bourrides flavored with saffron. That tastes very good, but the bourride loses its own distinctive flavor and begins to resemble a bouillabaisse instead. Our chef has preserved the singularity of this dish, which is always made with white fish, both those with firm flesh like conger eel or monkfish (also known as "sea devil") and fish of tender flesh, such as bream, John Dory, whiting, Mediterranean pandora fish, weever and gurnard. Sea bass or the sea dace could also be added. To make a special bourride for a festive occasion, you may even wish to use spiny lobster. If so, you will need two, each weighing 1 lb/500 g.

Also characteristic of bourride is the combination of fish stock with aïoli at the end, a definite hallmark of sunny Provence. The poet Mistral devoted his life to praising the beauty of his country and its language. In his journal, he wrote the word that, for him, epitomized all of Provence—simply, "Aïoli!"

So that you can imagine your heart in the South and your feet bathed by its waters, treat yourself and fellow bon vivants by preparing this opulent fisherman's bourride, evocative of all the combined fragrances of soil and sea.

Our wine expert's advice: a Muscadet sur lie.

2. Sauté the fish bones in a little of the olive oil. Add the sliced onion, shallot, thyme, bay leaf, a little coriander and the sprig of fennel. Salt and pepper lightly, and pour in water to cover. Add 2 cloves of garlic and cook over low heat.

3. Crush the remaining garlic into a paste. In a saucepan, whisk 1 egg yolk and 1 tbsp lukewarm water into the garlic. Cut the potatoes in thick slices.

4. To make the aïoli, drizzle the peanut oil into the garlic paste while whisking, as if to make mayonnaise. Place the potatoes in another saucepan, cover them with the fish stock and cook until just tender.

à la Provençal

5. *Chop and sauté the remaining onion in olive oil. Place the firm-fleshed fish in a saucepan, then strain the fish stock through a fine sieve and pour it in. Cook about 6 minutes. Add the other fish and cook, covered, another 4 minutes. Arrange the fish and potatoes on a serving platter.*

6. *Set aside a little aïoli in a gravy boat. Add 4 egg yolks to the rest and whisk vigorously. Pour in the hot fish stock while whisking over heat, and stop cooking just as it comes to a boil. Rub 12 slices of baguette with garlic and fry briefly in olive oil. Pour on the aïoli and fish stock sauce and serve with the aïoli and the bread.*

Fried Sole with

1. Skin, gut and clean the soles, dip them in salted and peppered milk, then flour lightly. Trim the artichoke hearts and squeeze on some lemon juice, then cut the hearts into thin slices and sticks. Do the same with the button mushrooms.

Ingredients:
4 8¾-oz/250-g soles
2 artichoke hearts
1 lemon
3½ oz/100 g button mushrooms
5¼ oz/150 g string beans
10 tbsp/150 g butter
3½ tbsp/50 ml peanut oil
1 tbsp olive oil
2 shallots; 1 tomato
2 tbsp chopped parsley
6½ tbsp/100 ml Noilly vermouth
2 cups/500 ml fish stock (see basic recipe)
¾ cup/200 ml crème fraîche
5 basil leaves
salt and pepper

Serves 4
Preparation time 40 minutes
Cooking time 20 minutes
Difficulty: ★

A beautifully orchestrated meal deserves a fanfare when this dish sets it off to a brilliant start. The soles, which should be the freshest you can find, are prepared like sole *meunière*, by dipping the fish into salted and peppered milk then flouring. This makes them beautifully crisp and golden when they are fried. When you roll them in the flour, pat the fillets with both hands to finely and evenly coat them. They are then fried in a mixture of butter and peanut oil. When they are as golden as you wish, remove them from the frying pan. Dispose of the cooking oil and set the fish aside for later use.
The combination of sole with artichokes, button mushrooms, string beans and tomatoes, along with not one, but two creamy sauces with their fragrant hint of chopped basil, makes for a bouquet of rich and wonderfully diverse flavors.
Our chef promises a resounding success with this dish, one your guests will remember with pleasure.
Our wine expert suggests a Chablis.

2. Heat half of the butter and 2 tbsp peanut oil in a frying pan. Fry the soles 5 or 6 minutes on each side until golden. Place them on a serving platter and keep them hot.

3. Heat 3½ tbsp/50 g of the butter and the olive oil in a frying pan. Sauté the artichoke sticks for 1 minute, then add the button mushrooms and cook an additional 2 minutes.

4. Cut away the hard stalk remnants from the tomato, then seed and cut into small pieces. Chop the shallots and sauté them over low heat in a little butter. Place the artichoke and mushroom sticks on the soles.

5. Pour the vermouth into the saucepan with the shallots. Reduce briefly, then add the fish stock. Reduce the sauce to ⅔ of its original volume. Stir in the crème fraîche and the tomato. While stirring briskly, add the rest of the butter and mix in the chopped basil. Spoon onto the serving platter.

6. Garnish with sprigs of parsley and serve.

Eel

1. *Clean and finely chop the white part of the leek, and sauté in a saucepan with a little butter. Peel the onion and carrot and finely dice them. In a saucepan, soak the prunes in a little lukewarm water.*

Ingredients:
16 pieces of eel, weighing 1½ oz/40 g each
1 leek without greens
6½ tbsp/100 g butter
1 onion
1 carrot
8 large prunes
4 boiling onions
8 large button mushrooms
2 bottles Saumur
1 bouquet garni
salt, freshly ground pepper

Serves 4
Preparation time: 20 minutes
Cooking time: 35 minutes
Difficulty: ★

2. *Add the onion and carrot to the leek. Sauté.*

The French love of poetry and history extends to the culinary arts. Our chef, a poet of flavor, here gives us an ancient recipe vibrant with the harmonies of his native soil.
Glaze the boiling onions very gently without browning them. They should not be covered by the butter, but just resting in it. Simmer them until all liquid has evaporated. Cover the saucepan with aluminum foil so that the onions have time to cook without browning.
Instead of discarding the mushroom stems, wash and add them to the vegetables to give these a delicious flavor. Like the boiling onions, the vegetables should be cooked over low heat without browning.
After cutting the eel into short lengths, let it stand for an hour so that the flesh does not break open. If has been refrigerated, do not cook it at once: eel does not like sudden changes of temperature and needs to spend some ten minutes at room temperature.
Saumur is a village in the Loire valley. If the white table wine that is produced there from the chenin blanc grape is not available, a Savennières, produced in the same area, can be substituted. Boil the wine to remove its acidity before adding it to the eel.
This refined dish should be reserved for special dinners; your guests will be enchanted by such quality.
Wines made from the Gamay grape harmonize well with the rich and flavorful meat of the eel. Our wine expert recommends a Gamay d'Anjou.

3. *Peel the boiling onions and cook over low heat in a saucepan with some butter, a little water and a pinch of sugar until glazed. Season with salt and pepper.*

4. *Cut the stems from the mushrooms and blanch the caps in a little salted water. Add the pieces of eel and the mushroom stems to the vegetables.*

Angevin

5. Heat the Saumur wine in a separate pan and flambé it, then pour our over the eel pieces. Add the bouquet garni, salt and pepper. Simmer over gentle heat for about 20 minutes.

6. Arrange the pieces of eel on a serving platter and keep warm. Strain the cooking liquid through a fine sieve, then reduce to half its original volume. Whisk in the butter. Arrange the prunes, button mushrooms and boiling onions on the serving platter. Pour on the sauce and serve very hot.

Hake with

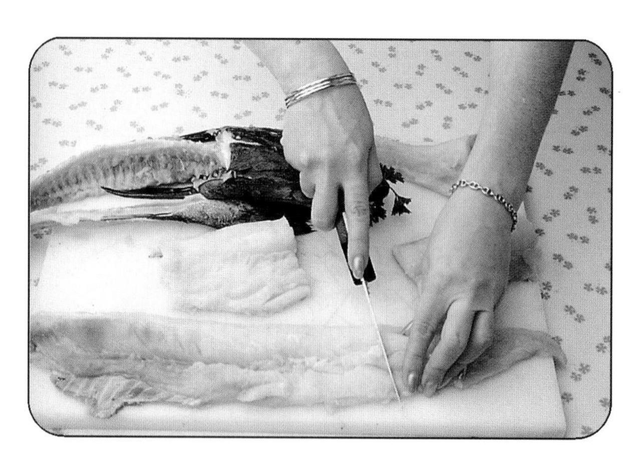

1. *Scale and fillet the fish (see basic recipe), and cut it into thin slices.*

Ingredients:
1 hake weighing 2 lb 3 oz/1 kg
15 small white onions
3 cups/750 ml white wine
1 bunch thyme
6½ tbsp/100 ml olive oil
6 tomatoes
1 lemon
salt and pepper

Serves 4
Preparation time: 10 minutes
Cooking time: 25 minutes
Difficulty: ✯

2. *Peel the boiling onions. Pour 2 cups/500 ml water and the white wine into a saucepan and bring to a boil. Add the thyme and the olive oil. Simmer over low heat.*

Here is a recipe that is somehow most suited to spring. Thyme, called *farigoule* in the Provençal dialect, and embodying the essence of the flora of the mountains of Provence, also imparts its fragrance to any house when used in cooking. This bountiful plant flourishes on dry, rocky hills and provides nectar to the many bees that visit. The ancient Greeks used it as an offering to nymphs and the goddess Venus, and the Romans already used it as a flavoring and condiment. In the Middle Ages, the delightful custom arose of embroidering a sprig of thyme with a bee on it onto the banner of a knight to remind the valiant warrior that the violence of war should never exclude gentleness.
The hake also loves the season when the first rays of sunlight reappear. Choose one with clear eyes, bright red rather than dark red gills, and firm flesh.
Your fish retailer can fillet the fish if you prefer not to do so yourself. The cooking time should be carefully adhered to, as hake does not benefit from extended cooking.
Hake with Thyme and Tomato is very simple, and can also be prepared with sole or whiting fillets. Broccoli and carrots form a delicious accompaniment with any of these fish. This spring dish should be served lukewarm, but can be reheated. It can also be enjoyed cold.
A mellow white wine will go best with this sauce. Discover the combination of Pouilly-Fuissé with a Saint-Véran.

3. *Add the small onions and season with salt and pepper. Cook until the onions are tender, then allow mixture to cool.*

4. *Place the hake fillets in a baking dish. Remove the thyme, then pour the cooled wine mixture over the fish.*

Thyme and Tomato

5. Peel, seed and dice the tomatoes. Add them to the hake fillets.

6. Add salt, pepper and lemon juice and cook 5 minutes over low heat on the stovetop. Serve warm or cold, as desired.

Sea Bass Scallops

1. *Clean and mince the shallots. Peel the potatoes. Cut them into little balls using a melon baller. Place the balls in water and set them aside.*

Ingredients:
1 sea bass weighing 2 lb 10 oz/1.2 kg
2 shallots
6 potatoes
4 tomatoes
½ cup/120 g butter
2 egg yolks
6½ tbsp/100 ml tarragon vinegar
juice of 1 lemon
1 bunch of tarragon
salt and pepper

Serves 4
Preparation time: 35 minutes
Cooking time: 20 minutes
Difficulty: ★ ★

2. *Peel, quarter and seed the tomatoes. Sauté the shallots in a little butter, being careful that they do not brown. Add the tomatoes. In a separate saucepan, fry the potato balls with some butter.*

Tarragon was introduced to Europe by returning crusaders. It spread quickly, and the gardener of King Louis the XIV regarded it as one of the best aromatic substances. Besides its qualities as an appetizer, an aid to digestion, a diuretic and a stimulant, tarragon is an excellent way to liven up salt-free diets such as those prescribed in the case of heart disease, hypertension or obesity.

This simple, fragrant and effective remedy can help people on such diets feel they are not being deprived at all. Its aroma and flavor, refined yet pungent, have given tarragon a prestigious position in the world of gastronomy.

Our chef prefers to cook sea bass in the summer, though tautog and monkfish also work well with this flavorful sabayon. Like all fish, they should be selected with care. Fillet and skin the bass, then cut it into four to six pieces. The cooking time should be exactly adhered to, as the flesh of the sea bass is delicate.

Make the sabayon over very low heat, whisking constantly to allow the egg yolks to thicken and become frothy without coagulating.

The accompaniments served with these scallops can be varied—button mushrooms, corn salad, or cress purée—experiment with the colors and pleasures of summer.

A Meursault Charmes, one of the fine white Burgundies, will bring the gentle flavor of tarragon and the iodized characteristics of sea bass into equilibrium with one another.

3. *To make the sabayon, combine the egg yolks, vinegar and a little water in a saucepan. Whisk continuously until smooth.*

4. *Place this mixture on the stove, over very low heat, while continuing to whisk. Add the lemon juice and chopped tarragon. Do not allow to boil.*

with Tarragon Sabayon

5. Pour the juice produced by the tomatoes in Step 2 into the sabayon, and beat until the sauce is creamy and thick. Season with salt and pepper.

6. Fry the sea bass scallops in a saucepan with the rest of the butter. Season with salt and pepper. Coat a serving platter with the sauce and arrange the bass on it. Serve accompanied by potato balls, steamed tomatoes and shreds of tarragon.

Pollack with

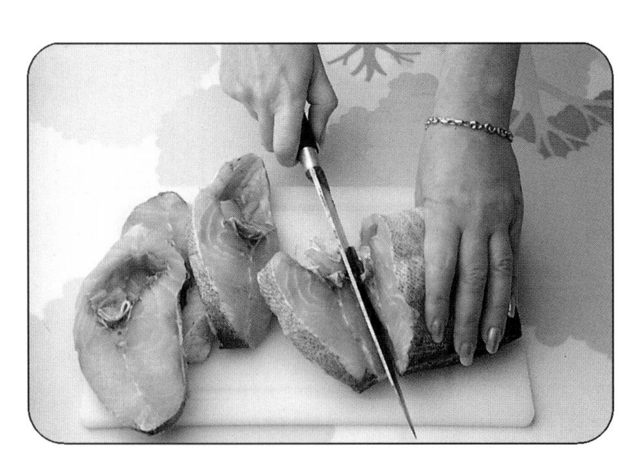

1. *Use scissors to remove the fins. Clean the pollack thoroughly and cut it into 4 slices.*

Ingredients:
1 pollack, weighing 2 lb 3 oz/1 kg
1 bunch of tarragon
½ cup/125 g butter
juice of 1 lemon
1 lb/500 g potatoes
oil
salt and pepper

Serves 6
Preparation time: 5 minutes
Cooking time: 25 minutes
Difficulty: ★

2. *Pluck the tarragon leaves and wash them thoroughly. Blend them with 6½ tbsp/100 g of the butter in a food processor. Season with salt and pepper and add the lemon juice.*

The pollack can attain a length of over three feet (one meter) and weigh up to 30 pounds (13.6 kg). It is found primarily in the Atlantic. The pollack is sold whole, in slices, in slabs or as fillets. The low fat content of its flesh makes it a lean fish, ideal for diets. Make sure it is fresh by checking that its flesh is glossy and its blood red. The hake, with a black back and light belly, is a close relative of the pollack and an excellent substitute. Halibut and burbot can also be used as variants of this recipe.
This dish is quick to prepare and sure to entrance you. Be careful; the fish does not benefit from prolonged cooking. Our chef's advice is to remove the skin. As you will discover, it comes away easily once the flesh is cooked. The potatoes also need to be cooked rapidly, or they will break up in the sauce.
For those days when you have had a rich dinner the evening before, Pollack with Tarragon, garnished with vegetables or a ragoût of white beet, will provide you with a light meal freshened by the flavor of tarragon.
Our wine expert suggests an Auxey-Duresses Blanc. This little village near Meursault is an excellent wine region that is too often neglected.

3. *Peel the potatoes and cut them into regular shapes.*

4. *Heat some oil in a saucepan. When the oil is hot, add the potatoes and fry them briefly.*

Tarragon

5. Pour in ½ glass of water and mix in the tarragon butter. Season to taste and cook over low heat.

6. Season the pieces of fish and fry them in the remaining butter and a little oil. Arrange the fish on a serving platter and serve together with the potatoes and tarragon butter sauce.

Tautog in

1. *Gut the tautog and remove the gills. Clean it thoroughly, but do not scale. Finely chop the onion.*

Ingredients:
1 tautog weighing 3 lb 3 oz/1.5 kg
1 onion
1 sprig of thyme
2 sprigs of parsley
juice of ½ lemon
4 lb 6 oz/2 kg rock salt
½ cup/125 g butter
table salt, pepper

Serves 5
Preparation time: 35 minutes
Cooking time: 10 minutes
Difficulty: ★

2. *Sprinkle some pepper into the tautog, then stuff it with the chopped onion, the thyme, parsley and a slice of lemon.*

This traditional recipe is a favorite of the fishermen of La Rochelle at the end of a good day's fishing.

In this method of preparation, the salt crust acts like buttered parchment paper, keeping in all the flavor of the fish. Our chef advises using rock salt if possible; it contains more iodine and the fish will gain in flavor. It also sticks better than normal table salt, and when you break the crust before serving, the skin of the tautog will come off easily with it. If you are obliged to use large-grained table salt, both the salt and the fish must be moistened so that they adhere well during cooking. The tautog should not be scaled: The scales protect the fish from the salt and retain the flavor. If using table salt, you will have to remove the skin while the fish is still hot.

To check how far the fish is cooked, pierce it through the crust with a needle. If the needle is warm to the touch upon withdrawing it, the fish is cooked. The tail needs special attention: To prevent it from burning, brush on some oil and wrap it in aluminum foil. If you want to eat the tautog hot, do not open up the crust directly upon removing the fish from the oven: The crust will keep the fish warm for half an hour, but reduce the cooking time by five minutes. Serve with fresh young vegetables of the season.

All scaly fishes can be prepared in this way and served as part of a cold buffet, where they are sure to be greatly appreciated.

This spectacular dish will be much enhanced by a fine bottle of wine. Choose a Mersault.

3. *Put a layer of rock salt on the bottom of a baking dish, then place the tautog on it and cover completely with rock salt.*

4. *Wrap the tail in a piece of aluminum foil to prevent it from burning, and bake the fish for approximately 35 minutes in a hot oven.*

Salt Crust

5. Add the lemon juice and a little salt and pepper to a saucepan containing approximately ⅓ cup/80 ml water. Bring to a boil, then whisk in the butter.

6. Just before serving, season the sauce lightly with salt and pepper and a little more lemon juice. Serve the tautog, with its salt crust removed, accompanied by this sauce.

Angler Fish

1. Fillet the angler fish (see basic recipe).

Ingredients:
1 angler fish,
2 lb 3 oz/1 kg
10 tbsp/150 g butter
7 oz/200 g fresh mushrooms or 3½ oz/100 g dried mushrooms
1 glass white wine
6½ tbsp/100 ml heavy cream
parsley
salt and pepper

Serves 6
Preparation time: 5 minutes
Cooking time: 20 minutes
Difficulty: ✶

2. Cut the fillets into scallops ⅜ in/1 cm thick, and beat them gently to break the fibers. Generously butter the baking dish.

The angler fish, also called monkfish, has been nicknamed "sea devil" because of its hideous head. But you will not see the head displayed at your fish retailer's; only the rest of the body is sold commercially. This fish has no small bones and no scales, and its backbone can be easily removed. The flesh is medium-fat and very easy to digest, and its iodine and phosphorus content make it recommended eating for everyone, especially convalescents.

Wild mushrooms can be picked much of the year, but be very careful: take only mushrooms you can positively identify as edible. Well-stocked grocery stores offer several varieties: oyster mushrooms in autumn, chanterelles from June to October, and many more.

To make sure the fish scallops remain flat without curling up, our chef advises you to lay a piece of paper on top of them and beat them to break the fibers. Zucchini sautéed with garlic make a choice accompaniment.

Serve very hot and enjoy Angler Fish with Mushrooms without delay.

Our wine expert feels that the refined flavor of the mushrooms requires a fine wine with vegetal aroma. He recommends a Savennières (Clos du Papillon).

3. Arrange the angler fish scallops in the baking dish. Sprinkle with salt and pepper, then the mushrooms.

4. Combine the wine with a glass of water and pour over the scallops. Bake them in a medium oven for about 10 minutes.

with Mushrooms

5. Remove the angler fish scallops and mushrooms to a serving platter and keep them hot.

6. Reduce the liquid from the baking pan to half its original volume. Add the heavy cream, let it thicken for several minutes, and adjust the seasoning. Pour this sauce, very hot, over the angler fish scallops just before serving.

Sole

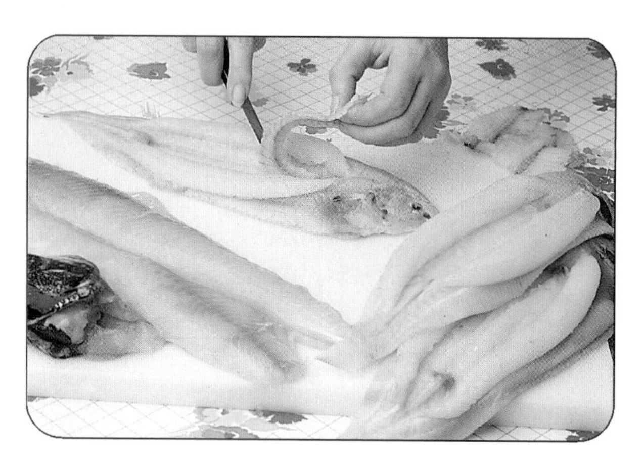

1. Clean the soles and remove the black skin. Remove the backbone, being careful not to pierce the underside of the sole.

Ingredients:
4 small soles
1 lb/450 g pike fillet
1 clove garlic
2 eggs
2 cups/500 g crème fraîche
2 shallots
1 glass white wine
1 cup/250 ml fish stock (see basic recipe)
3½ tbsp/50 g butter
salt, cayenne pepper

Serves 4
Preparation time: 1 hour
Cooking time: 25 minutes
Difficulty: ★ ★ ★

2. For the filling, purée the pike flesh in a food processor. Add the garlic and season with salt and cayenne pepper.

Roman gastronomes loved sole and gave it the name "Jupiter's sandal." Louis XIV made it a royal dish, and from the 19th century onwards, all the finest chefs employed their best talents in preparing it.

The best known variety is the sole caught in the English Channel and the Atlantic, the North Sea and the Baltic Sea.

The pike, called "sea wolf" in the Middle Ages, provides exquisite meat for the stuffing. You could use walleye, another freshwater fish, or whiting caught in the Atlantic, with its delicate, flaky flesh; it is also moderately priced. Another alternative it to use a fish with pink flesh, like salmon or salmon trout, which may be enhanced with spinach or fresh cress for an additional visual element.

The most difficult step is removing the backbone from the sole. You need a good knife and a lot of dexterity to avoid damaging the fragile meat and tearing the white skin.

You can slice lobster tail and place it on top of the sole as an accompaniment, as you see in the picture, or our chef suggests aubergine caviar as another option. Decorate the sole with truffle and serve it hot.

Our wine expert advises selecting a fine bottle of white Burgundy to accompany this festive dish. He proposes a Puligny-Montrachet Les Folatières.

3. Add the eggs and blend the mixture for 30 seconds.

4. Add 1¼ cups/300 ml of the crème fraîche and blend until the stuffing mixture is smooth.

Soufflé

5. Using a pastry bag, fill the soles with the stuffing. Chop the shallots. Butter a baking dish and sprinkle in the shallots. Place the soles in the baking dish.

6. Pour the white wine and fish stock over the fish and cook 5 minutes in a hot oven. Place the soles on a serving platter. Reduce the remaining liquid to half its original volume, add the remaining crème fraîche, and let thicken. Whisk in the butter. Strain the sauce through a sieve and serve with the soles.

Brill Soufflé

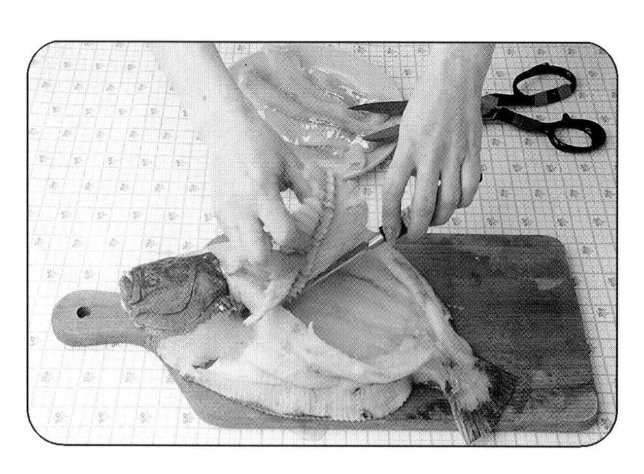

1. *Open up the brill from the top and remove the backbone (see basic recipe). Fillet the whiting and remove the skin.*

Ingredients:
1 brill weighing 2 lb 10 oz/1.2 kg
8 crayfish
7 oz/200 g whiting fillets
2 eggs
2 cups/500 ml heavy cream
2 large onions
2 carrots
1 bouquet garni
1 bunch parsley stalks
⅔ cup/150 ml fish stock (see basic recipe)
¾ cup/200 ml Nantua sauce (see basic recipe)
salt and pepper

Serves 4
Preparation time: 1 hour 10 minutes
Cooking time: 20 minutes
Difficulty: ★ ★ ★

2. *Make a fish mousse by puréeing the whiting fillets thoroughly in a food processor.*

In French cuisine, the word *cardinal* denotes fish dishes or sauces using lobster, and refers to the color the lobster turns when cooked. The brill—with its delicate, lean, white, nutritious flesh—resembles the turbot, but costs less. You will be required to perform a delicate operation: removing the backbone without ruining the fillets. This job requires considerable dexterity. A good sharp knife will enable you to slice open the backbone along its entire length without damaging the fillet. It can then be removed, carefully, using the tip of a paring knife.
The fish mousseline can be enhanced by a mirepoix of onions, carrots, and shallots. If some of the fish mousse is left over, you can make quenelles poached in salted water. Accompanied by a tomato sauce, these will provide a second course or a complementary dish to the brill. For variety, this recipe can also be made using turbot and sole. Do remember, however, that larger fish require more time to cook.
Although a roasting bag has a certain elegance, it is only there to prevent the fish from falling aparat when lifting it out of the baking dish after cooking. Do not forget to remove it. Fish soufflé is always served upside down so that it does not collapse just as you are about to put it on the table.
Accompanied by beans or broccoli, Brill Soufflé Cardinal will delight everyone. Our wine expert recommends a Riesling.

3. *Add the eggs, season with salt and pepper, and blend together for several seconds.*

4. *Pour in the heavy cream, emulsify the fish mousse and put aside in a cool place. Peel and chop the onions and carrots and place them in a baking dish, then add the bouquet garni and parsley stalks.*

Cardinal

5. Slit open a roasting bag and place the brill on it. Stuff the brill with the fish mousse, then fold the flaps of skin over the mousse to close it.

6. Pour in the fish stock and cook for about 20 minutes in a low oven. In the meantime, poach the crayfish and make a Nantua sauce according to the basic recipe. When done, arrange the brill on a serving platter, accompanied by the crayfish and Nantua sauce.

Skate Cheeks

1. *Finely chop the tarragon, chives and parsley. Clean and cut the white part of the leeks into thin shreds.*

Ingredients:
2 lb 3 oz/1 kg skate cheeks
1 sprig tarragon
chives
parsley
2 leeks
¾ cup/200 ml white wine
6½ tbsp/100 ml fish stock (see basic recipe) or 1 fish stock cube
½ tsp/2 g saffron
4 tomatoes
1 bouquet garni
2 cups/500 ml cream
5 tbsp/70 g butter
salt and pepper

Serves 5
Preparation time: 20 minutes
Cooking time: 20 minutes
Difficulty: ★

2. *Pour the white wine over the skate cheeks and bring to a boil. Dissolve the fish stock cube in 6½ tbsp/100 ml water.*

Camille Cerf was the president of the "*Club des Cent*" in the 1920s. He often dined at the famous Larue restaurant on the Place de la Madeleine, and the chef, Patron Duplat, named this dish after the great gastronome.
Ask your fish retailer specifically for deboned cheeks. You will not find skate cheeks on display, but your request will identify you as a connoisseur and gourmet: This part of the fish is much sought after by food lovers.
Do not cook the skate cheeks too long; one minute for each side is enough. Our chef has chosen saffron, but if you prefer more exotic flavors, he suggests trying curry. The tarragon provides a refreshing aroma, giving your sauce an original touch.
As accompaniment, our chef suggests chicory sautéed in butter. Angler fish cheeks will also go well with this sauce. They are similar to those of the skate, but keep better. Langoustines are also delicious prepared this way. This venerable dish, which is not at all common, will put its gastronomic stamp on your dinner and elevate you to the status of a cordon-bleu chef.
The sweetness of the tarragon, the bitterness of the chicory and the tender succulence of the skate cheeks require a harmonizing influence in the form of a dry white wine, lively and full of fruit. Our wine expert recommends a Sancerre Blanc.

3. *After letting the skate cheeks boil for a minute, pour in the fish bouillon or stock. Salt lightly and add pepper.*

4. *Sprinkle the skate cheeks with the saffron and cook for 2 minutes.*

à la Camille Cerf

5. Peel, seed and chop the tomatoes, then add them to the skate cheeks along with the bouquet garni. Remove from heat, take out the skate cheeks and put them aside.

6. Add the cream, the chopped herbs and the shredded leek to the cooking liquid, and reduce the sauce over low heat. Whisk in the butter. When the sauce has thickened, pour it over the skate cheeks, briefly bring to a boil, and serve.

Pike Quenelles

1. For the panade, bring the milk to a boil. Add the butter and flour and whisk vigorously to eliminate any lumps. When it has a fairly dry consistency, add the egg and a pinch of salt. Stir again and set aside.

Ingredients:
10½ oz/300 g pike flesh
pinch of nutmeg
2 eggs
2 egg whites
13 tbsp/200 g butter
1½ cups/350 ml Nantua sauce (see basic recipe)
salt and pepper
For the panade:
1 cup/250 ml milk
5 tsp/25 g butter
¾ cup/85 g flour
1 egg
salt

Serves 4
Preparation time: 40 minutes
Cooking time: 15 minutes
Chilling time: 12 hours
Difficulty: ★ ★ ★

Succulent quenelles, with their subtle, delicate flavor, are a very refined part of French cuisine. Their popularization in canteens everywhere has done them a grave disservice, as the delicate poached dumplings do not take well to mass production. This recipe will help restore your faith, and our chef invites you to partake of a refined delight.
To start with, choose the pike with care: The eyes will be clear if the fish is fresh. Chill the pike flesh before puréeing it. Take care with it, as it is the most important ingredient in the quenelles.
The panade should have a dry consistency; removing as much moisture as possible from it will keep the dough light. When the mixture is ready, put it aside for twelve hours to become firm. You will then have no difficulty forming the quenelles.
The dumplings will swell when poached: Serve them without delay as soon as they have reached their maximum size.
Pike Quenelles with Nantua Sauce is a wonderful way of celebrating a fine catch, if there are fishers in your circle of friends and family. To honor their success, open up a fine white burgundy. Our wine expert suggests a Meursault-Genevrières.

2. If necessary, fillet the pike (see basic recipe) and remove the bones. When the flesh has chilled, purée it. Mix in the panade, then season with the nutmeg, salt and pepper.

3. Add the whole eggs. Blend, then add the egg whites. Blend once more until the mixture is smooth.

4. Clarify the butter. When it has cooled, add it gradually, while blending constantly. Put the quenelle mixture in the refrigerator to chill for 12 hours.

with Nantua Sauce

5. Break off pieces of the quenelle mixture and roll them in flour to give them the desired shape.

6. Bring a saucepan of water to a boil and poach the quenelles. Heat the Nantua sauce. Arrange the quenelles on a serving dish, pour the sauce over them, and serve accompanied by poached crayfish.

Red Mullet on a

1. Bring a saucepan of salted water to a boil. Clean and wash the potatoes thoroughly, and boil them in their jackets.

Ingredients:
6 red mullet, weighing 6¼-14 oz/180-400 g each
4 good quality potatoes
3½ tbsp/50 g butter
3½ tbsp/50 ml olive oil
1 bunch flat-leaf parsley
salt, freshly ground pepper
For the vinaigrette:
4 tsp/20 ml sherry vinegar
⅓ cup/80 ml olive oil
salt and pepper

Serves 4
Preparation time: 20 minutes
Cooking time: 25 minutes
Difficulty: ★

2. Fillet the red mullet. Remove the small bones with the help of tweezers. Put the fillets aside.

Red mullet is an exquisite member of the mullet family of fish, caught in Vendée and the region around Cherbourg. It is rich in protein, phosphorus and iodine, low in calories, and easy to digest. Their skin is pink with golden stripes, and the first dorsal fin has black spots. In Europe it is available from February to June. It may be difficult to obtain in North America, but sea bass is also suitable for this dish, as is salmon, a fish that will do your table honor.

Red Mullet on a Bed of Potatoes is a delicious fish recipe, quick and easy to prepare. It is so simple that you will love it for the pleasure it gives you with such little effort. By now you know how fish fillets are prepared. All the bones must be carefully removed.

The vinaigrette should be made using olive oil; mullet deserves this special treatment. Our chef recommends a sherry vinegar with a subtle aroma.

For our wine expert, a fine wine grown near the ocean is necessary to create a symbiosis between the ingredients called for here. He suggests a white Graves wine, for example a Château Fieuzal.

3. When the potatoes are cooked, let them cool a little, then cut them into rounds.

4. Melt the butter in a frying pan and cook the potato rounds in it, taking care not to burn them. Add a little salt and pepper.

Bed of Potatoes

5. Prepare the vinaigrette with the sherry vinegar, olive oil, and some salt and pepper.

6. Fry the mullet in olive oil over high heat for about 30 seconds on each side. Keep them hot. Place 6-8 warm potato slices on each plate, and arrange 3 small fillets of mullet on top of them. Pour on 2 tbsp of vinaigrette, garnish with parsley, and serve.

Mussels

Ingredients:
2 lb 3 oz/1 kg mussels
3 shallots
1 glass dry white wine
3½ tbsp/50 g butter
1 tbsp flour
1 tbsp tomato paste
2 sprigs parsley
1 tbsp Armagnac
8 slices white bread
salt and pepper

Serves 4
Preparation time: 25 minutes
Cooking time: 20 minutes
Difficulty: ✯

1. Clean and wash the mussels thoroughly. Finely chop the shallots. Cook the mussels in a saucepan with the shallots and white wine just until they open.

2. Retain the cooking liquid left by the mussels. Break them open and keep them hot.

In Bordeaux, people are attached to their vineyards. Wine spreads its benefits like a good minister, and rare are those dishes that are not flavored by fine, full-bodied, balanced wines—wines full of character and aroma.
Joining together shallots, parsley and wine makes a sauce *à la bordelaise*, and the tomato in this recipe gives it a regional touch.
Our chef is partial to boudot mussels because of their ideal small size, generous flesh, and outstanding aroma. *Boudots* are oak stakes complete with the bark of the tree, approximately six meters (just over six yards) long, which are driven halfway into the ground to form an enclosure that is then filled with young mussels. They are cultivated intensively from Cotentin to Charente, and the boudots give the mussels their name.
If boudot mussels are not available, any small mussel will do, or you can substitute clams. You will enjoy their refined flavor *à la bordelaise*, as well.
This is a colorful and aromatic dish, and an original way of cooking mussels. The recipe is easy to make and always works: Your success is assured. What is more, it is suitable for dieters, nutritionally balanced, and rich in iodine and phosphorus.
Our wine expert believes the white wines in the Graves region have been too often neglected. Remarkably balanced, they provide the perfect accompaniment to mussels. He recommends a Château-Carbonnieux Blanc.

3. Make a roux with the butter and flour.

4. Add the tomato paste to the roux, combine well, then strain the mussels' cooking liquid through a sieve and pour it in.

à la Bordelaise

5. Bring the sauce to a boil and adjust the seasoning if necessary. Chop the parsley; add it and the Armagnac to the sauce. Pour the sauce over the mussels.

6. Cut out heart-shaped pieces of bread and serve them as an accompaniment to the mussels, which should be served very hot.

Stuffed Sardines

1. Peel and finely chop the shallots; chop the mushrooms as well. Remove the backbone of the sardines with the aid of a small knife.

Ingredients:
16 sardines
5¼ oz/150 g shallots
6½ tbsp/100 ml olive oil
4 button mushrooms
2 eggs
4 sprigs parsley
2 cloves garlic
thyme
salt and pepper

Serves 4
Preparation time: 40 minutes
Cooking time: 15 minutes
Difficulty: ★

2. Fry the shallots in a frying pan with some of the olive oil, then add the mushrooms.

Sardines are readily available all year round; they are also simple to prepare and inexpensive. Because they are so easy to prepare, like all simple things, sardines are far too little regarded. They are popular of course, but they deserve better than just that! They come to your fish retailer from the Atlantic and the Mediterranean. They are rich in sulfur, vitamins B2 and B6, calcium and phosphorus, and are easy to digest.
Fresh anchovies from the Mediterranean, which are small and delicately flavored, could be substituted for them.
This recipe is uncomplicated. The presentation of the sardines with the tail folded over toward the head will demand a little concentration at first, but it will quickly become child's play.
This is a first course that can be enjoyed as part of a buffet, as hors-d'oeuvres, or at a barbecue. They can be eaten hot or at room temperature, and will be one of summer's greatest pleasures for everyone.
For our wine expert, a Bellet Blanc, which comes from the vineyards overlooking Nice, is the perfect companion to this sardine recipe from the south of France.

3. While cooking the shallots and mushrooms, hard-boil the eggs, then shell and finely chop them.

4. Add the eggs to the fried mushrooms and shallots. Chop the parsley and garlic and add them to this mixture. Season with a little salt and pepper.

Niçoises

5. Cook the stuffing mixture for another 2 minutes. Fill each of the sardines with 1 tbsp of the stuffing and close them by tucking the tail just under the head.

6. Place the sardines in a baking dish. Pour the rest of the olive oil over them and sprinkle with thyme. Salt and pepper, and cook in a hot oven for 5 minutes.

Stuffed Crabs

1. *Poach the crabs in a pot of boiling water. Add salt and a pinch of Cayenne pepper. Chop the shallots, garlic and parsley.*

Ingredients:
4 crabs, each 10½ oz/300 g
1 pinch Cayenne pepper
3 shallots
2 cloves garlic
parsley
cooking oil
3½ oz/100 g porcini
5¼ oz/150 g ham
1 glass dry white wine
1¾ cups/200 g dried white bread crumbs
4 tsp/20 g butter
salt and pepper

Serves 4
Preparation time: 1 hour 30 minutes
Cooking time: 35 minutes
Difficulty: ★ ★

2. *After cooking for 15 minutes, take the crabs out of the water, then remove the meat from the shells, saving them for later use.*

Inspired by the stuffed crabs of West Indian cuisine after a culinary sojourn in Guadeloupe, our chef created a French-style stuffing based on porcini, ham and shallots. Any mushroom will do, button mushrooms for example, but the flavor of porcini harmonizes particularly well with that of crabmeat.

The common edible crab is the largest European crab. It lives on rocky or pebbly seabed, and is caught just as often in the Atlantic as in the Mediterranean. Spring is the main season for it, and it should be available at a reasonable price then.

The first pair of legs with two large pincers is very well developed and contains such delicious meat that in Quebec the common edible crab is cultivated just for its pincers!

The only demanding aspect of this recipe, which is otherwise simple to prepare, is taking time to remove the flesh from the shell. In this way you will obtain a natural vessel with a deep cavity for the stuffing.

Instead of the common edible crab you can use spider crab, considered by some to be the finest of all crustaceans.

Stuffed Crabs à la Chef will warm the heart and appetite of any guests. It is a good dish for business dinners, one which will gain the gratitude of your guests and win them over. It would also lend a marine touch to a rustic buffet.

Our wine expert feels that the combination of the Sauvignon grape variety with crabmeat constitutes a marriage of like minds. He advises you to choose a Sancerre Blanc.

3. *Heat 3½ tbsp/50 ml oil in a frying pan and sauté first the shallots, then the garlic and finally the parsley.*

4. *Mince the porcini and chop the ham. Sauté them with the crab meat in a separate pan with some oil. Add salt and pepper, then mix in the shallots, garlic and parsley mixture.*

à la Chef

5. Pour in the white wine. Mix in most of the bread-crumbs (reserve some for the garnish) and cook 15 minutes over low heat.

6. Fill the crab shells with this mixture and sprinkle with the remaining breadcrumbs. Add a dollop of butter. Bake in the oven, garnish, and serve hot.

Curried

1. *Peel and finely chop the shallots.*

Ingredients:
24 large shrimp tails
3 shallots
3 tbsp oil
1 tsp curry powder
1 cup/250 ml
heavy cream
1 glass white wine
3½ tbsp/50 ml
Cognac
1 tomato
salt and pepper

Serves 4
Preparation time: 20 minutes
Cooking time: 15 minutes
Difficulty: ★

2. *Shell the shrimp and sauté them in very hot oil over high heat. Season with salt and pepper.*

If you have ever had the pleasure of combing the beach after the tide has gone out with your trousers rolled up, and armed with a net, you will have seen the shrimp jumping away to escape being caught. There are, of course, many varieties of shrimp and they can be bought all year long. This recipe can also be made substituting prawns or crayfish.
When purchasing shrimp, check to see if their eyes are still protruding. If not, the shrimp are no longer fresh.
Our chef advises you to fry the shrimp quickly, or they will soften.
The unusual addition of curry, normally reserved for lamb dishes, gives this dish a surprise effect, which is what this recipe is all about.
Our wine expert tells us that curry goes well with Alsatian wines. Drink a Gewürztraminer, a marvelous *grand cru*.

3. *Remove the shrimp from the frying pan and put them aside. Sauté the shallots in the same pan.*

4. *Return the shrimp to the pan and sprinkle with the curry powder. Cook again for 2 minutes.*

Shrimp

5. Pour in the cream, white wine and Cognac, and allow to gently simmer.

6. Arrange the shrimp tails on a serving platter. Strain the sauce through a fine sieve, then add the skinned, seeded and chopped tomato. Simmer for a few moments, then pour the sauce over the shrimp and serve them very hot.

Walleye in

1. *Peel and finely chop the shallots.*

Ingredients:
1 walleye weighing
3 lb 5 oz /1.5 kg
4 shallots
13 tbsp/200 g butter
1¼ cups/300 ml good red wine
1 cup/250 ml fish stock (see basic recipe)
⅔ cup/150 ml heavy cream
salt and pepper

Serves 4
Preparation time: 20 minutes
Cooking time: 30 minutes
Difficulty: ★

2. *Sauté most of the chopped shallots in a little butter over gentle heat, then pour in ¾ of the red wine. Add a little salt and pepper and reduce the mixture to ¼ its original volume over low heat.*

A near relation of the perch, the walleye is a winter fish with delicate, firm white flesh. As is always the case with fish, make sure it is fresh before you buy it. The eyes should be protruding; if they are sunken, the walleye is not fresh. You can also make this recipe with perch or pike. Another variation is to poach the walleye in white wine, rather than red, and to make a *beurre blanc* instead of the *beurre rouge*, or red butter sauce.

Our chef recommends that you choose a quality red wine for this dish; an ordinary one will make the sauce sour. Reduce the sauce well before adding the butter. The butter should be fairly soft; keep it at room temperature.

Serve the walleye hot as soon as the sauce is ready, because it cannot be reheated. Our chef suggests steamed potatoes or rice as accompaniments.

The very refined Walleye in Beurre Rouge should be reserved for exceptional occasions. Since the walleye is at home in the rough waters of the Loire, our wine expert advises you to choose a fine wine from this region, a Chinon or a Sancerre Blanc.

3. *Fillet the walleye, remove the skin, and slice the flesh into 4 good portions.*

4. *Grease the baking dish with butter and sprinkle in the uncooked shallots. Place the fish in the dish, add salt and pepper, and cover with the rest of the wine and the fish stock. Cook in a moderate oven for 10 minutes.*

Beurre Rouge

5. When the red wine and shallot mixture has been reduced, add the heavy cream and simmer.

6. Arrange the walleye on the serving platter. Whip the butter into the sauce. Adjust the seasoning and pour the sauce over the fish. Serve very hot.

Brill with

1. *Combine the walleye and 4 shelled oysters in a food processor and blend to make a very smooth purée. Add the egg and 6½ tbsp/100 ml of the crème fraîche, and season with salt and pepper. Strain the purée through a fine sieve and refrigerate.*

Ingredients:
1 brill and 1 small walleye, filleted
12 oysters
1 egg
1¼ cups/300 ml crème fraîche
14 oz/400 g carrots
1 lb/500 g cucumbers
2 shallots
6½ tbsp/100 g butter
1½ cups/350 ml vermouth
1½ cups/350 ml fish stock (see basic recipe)
3½ oz/100 g spinach
nutmeg
1 bunch of cress
salt and pepper

Serves 4
Preparation time: 1 hour 30 minutes
Cooking time: 35 minutes
Difficulty: ★ ★ ★

Brill has delicate and mild flesh, as exquisite or nearly so as that of the turbot, and is fairly inexpensive. Well prepared, it will enchant you with its subtle flavor.

When preparing the vegetables, remember that carrots need to cook longer than cucumber. Blanch the carrots for a few moments before adding the cucumber, letting the strips become soft enough to be manipulated for the final steps in this recipe. Dip the cucumber in cold water to keep it green.

Before wrapping the brill fillets in plastic wrap, put a piece of aluminum foil under them so that it comes a little up the sides. This will prevent the plastic wrap from sticking to the strips of vegetables while cooking, enabling you to remove it easily and avoiding any unpleasant surprises while arranging your dish.

Do not add the cress purée to the sauce until you are ready to serve. If you add it too soon, the sauce will take on a grayish hue. You should also squeeze on a little lemon juice when the cress is cooked so that it retains its color.

When everything is ready, you will have to acknowledge that the scrupulous work has been worth the effort. Your guests are sure to be dumbfounded by this spectacular presentation. Our wine expert recommends a Rully Blanc. This far too little-known wine deserves to be brought out of hiding.

2. *Open the remaining oysters. Slice the carrots and cucumbers into thin strips, blanch them briefly in salted water, and let cool. Thinly slice the brill. Lay each slice on a piece of plastic wrap, cover with a thin layer of the purée, and place 2 oysters on it. Finally, cover with another slice of brill.*

3. *Sprinkle the brill lightly with salt and pepper. Apply alternating strips of carrot and cucumber, place a small piece of foil on top of each, and then enclose firmly in the plastic wrap.*

4. *Sauté the chopped shallots in butter. Pour in the vermouth and reduce its volume by half, then add the water from the oysters. Strain and reduce the fish stock. Blanch the spinach and season it with nutmeg, salt and pepper.*

Oyster Stuffing

5. Combine the reduced vermouth and stock, season lightly and add the rest of the crème fraîche. Return to the heat and let the mixture thicken again. Cook the cress leaves in salted water for 3 minutes. Drain them, squeeze out excess water, and purée in a food processor. Strain through a fine sieve.

6. Steam the stuffed brill packages in a double boiler for about 15 minutes. Add the puréed cress to the sauce, bring it to a boil, and whisk in the remaining butter. Pour over the serving platter. Remove the plastic wrap and foil from the stuffed brill and serve with the blanched spinach.

Walleye with Caramelized

1. Peel and finely dice the carrot, onion and garlic. Combine them in a saucepan with the Anjou wine, the bouquet garni and the chervil.

Ingredients:

1 walleye weighing 1 lb 10½ oz/800 g
12 langoustines
1 carrot
1 onion
1 clove of garlic
4½ cups/1 liter Anjou wine
1 bouquet garni
1 bunch of chervil
6½ tbsp/100 g sugar
3 tbsp brown sugar
2 leeks
7 oz/200 g tagliatelle
13 tbsp/200 g butter
salt and pepper

Serves 4
Preparation time: 20 minutes
Cooking time: 45 minutes
Difficulty: ★

2. Mix in the sugar. Season with salt and pepper, then add 1 tbsp of the brown sugar.

The name of this dish seems to promise a lot, and when you prepare it you are sure to agree that its elegance is worthy of such a beautiful title. This recipe is suitable for all fishes with strongly-flavored flesh, for example brill or pike.

Our chef offers these suggestions: Add only pepper to the langoustines before wrapping them in the leeks, as the iodized flavor of these crustaceans does not require additional salt. Put a drop of oil on the pasta after removing it from the water to prevent it from sticking together.

Another piece of advice: To make sure your sauce succeeds, reduce it to half its original volume, cook the vegetables and reduce once more until the desired consistency is reached. Only then should the butter be added.

Those lucky enough to live in an area with lots of ponds will have no problems obtaining walleye. Walleye with Caramelized Leeks and Langoustines is a deliciously refined recipe that will enchant your guests.

Only a fine white Burgundy can reach the same heights as this special, festive dish. Our wine expert therefore recommends a Puligny-Montrachet.

3. Bring 2 saucepans of salted water to a boil. Cut the white parts of the leeks into 3-in/7-cm lengths. Blanch the leeks in one saucepan and cook the tagliatelle in the other.

4. Fillet the walleye and then cut it into slices. Shell the tails of the langoustines and, once the leeks have cooled, roll up the tail meat in single layers of leek.

Leeks and Langoustines

5. Heat 2 frying pans. In a little butter, fry the slices of walleye, lightly dusted with salt and pepper. Sprinkle the prawn tails with the remaining brown sugar and cook them in the other pan. Let them caramelize slightly.

6. Strain the seasoned wine from Step 1 through a fine sieve and finish the sauce by whisking in the rest of the butter. Arrange a bouquet of tagliatelle, 3 slices of walleye and 3 prawn rolls on each serving plate. Pour on the sauce and serve.

Cunner with

1. *Peel and finely chop 5 of the shallots. Heat some olive oil in a saucepan, and sauté the fennel seeds and chopped shallots over very gentle heat.*

Ingredients:
2 cunners, each
1 lb 3 oz/500 g
6 shallots
¾ cup/200 ml olive oil
½ tsp fennel seeds
3 tomatoes
basil leaves
pinch of sugar
1 oz/30 g black olives
2 tbsp/30 g butter
1 oz/30 g sesame
seeds, roasted
salt and pepper

Serves 4
Preparation time: 45 minutes
Cooking time: 40 minutes
Difficulty: ★ ★

2. *Finely chop the remaining shallot and cut the tomatoes into quarters. Cook them and the basil leaves in a little olive oil in a second saucepan. Add salt and pepper. Pour in a glass of water, add a pinch of sugar and simmer over gentle heat.*

No, you haven't picked up the wrong book. In spite of the sweet-sounding title, this is not a chocolate cake, but a fish recipe! The sesame seeds make a crusty topping and, in concert with the olive oil, tomato and chopped olives, give this dish its flavorful Mediterranean character.
When blending the shallot sauce, make sure there is always some liquid there to bind it. The sauce should be yellow and fluid.
Use no more than a scant teaspoon of fennel seeds. If you add more than this, the powerful fennel flavor will dominate, and destroy the balance of this dish.
Our chef recommends zucchini as an accompaniment with this meal, which cannot be reheated. It must be eaten right away "because," he says, "like a beautiful woman, it doesn't like to be kept waiting!"
The Bandol is an elegant wine. Follow the advice of our wine expert and enjoy a Bandol Blanc de Blanc.

3. *When the tomato sauce is cooked, blend it and set it aside. Blend the shallot, fennel seed and olive oil mixture with a hand mixer.*

4. *Seed and chop the black olives. Whisk 1 tbsp butter into the shallot and fennel seed mixture, and add the chopped black olives. Season with salt and pepper. Whisk 1 tbsp butter into the tomato sauce as well. Adjust the seasoning.*

Sesame Seed Crust

5. Scale and fillet the cunners (see basic recipe). Season the fillets lightly with salt and pepper and cover the skin with roasted sesame seeds. Heat the remaining olive oil in an ovenproof dish.

6. Place the cunner fillets in the dish and bake about 10 minutes in a hot oven. Cover the bottom of a serving platter with the tomato sauce, then decorate the edge with the shallot purée. Arrange the fish on the platter and serve hot.

Salmon

1. *Remove the rind and cartilage from the bacon and cut it into small cubes. Soak the lentils.*

Ingredients:
1 lb 12 oz/800 g salmon fillets
3½ oz/100 g slab bacon
14 oz/400 g lentils
1 onion
4 carrots
1 whole clove
1 clove garlic
½ cup/120 g butter
1 bouquet garni
1 bunch of chives
salt and pepper

Serves 4
Preparation time: 20 minutes
Cooking time: 1 hour
Difficulty: ✭

2. *Peel and finely chop the onion. Peel the carrots and stick the clove into the clove of garlic. Fry half of the bacon cubes in a saucepan with a little butter; reserve the other half.*

Though this combination might strike you as somewhat surprising at first glance, the exquisite taste of lentils is being rediscovered. What is more, they offer good nutritional value, being rich in iron and phosphorus without excessive callories.
The salmon fillets should be sliced in the center, and only fried on one side.
It is possible to fry the salmon fillets in advance; just place them on the hot lentils and reheat the dish as a whole in the oven for one or two minutes before serving.
So that the lentils cook more quickly, soak them for several hours previously, or cook them gently in a copious amount of water. Salt slows down the cooking process considerably, so it should only be added at the end.
The bacon should be cooked first. It will give up its fat, allowing you to fry the onions in it and lending the lentils an absolutely irresistible smoky flavor.
This dish will have a great future: You will certainly be asked to make it again.
The excellent combination of salmon and Sauvignon will be confirmed again with this dish. Our wine expert suggests a Pouilly-Fumé.

3. *Add the chopped onion, carrots and the bouquet garni to the fried bacon and stir.*

4. *Pour in the lentils. Cover with water and cook over low heat for about 40 minutes.*

with Lentils

5. Cut pieces of salmon fillet about ¾ in/2 cm thick. Slice them open ¾ of the way through along their length, then open and flatten them slightly.

6. When ready to serve, spoon the lentils onto a serving platter. Put a little salt and pepper on the salmon slices and fry them, on one side only, in a little butter. Arrange them on the lentils. Decorate with sticks of chives and the rest of the bacon.

Scallops of

1. Peel the potatoes and cut them into boat-shaped pieces. Halve them lengthwise and hollow them out using a melon baller.

Ingredients:
1 sea bass weighing
2 lbs 10 oz/1.2 kg
4 potatoes
6 shallots
1 tbsp savory
2 cloves garlic
10 coriander seeds
3 basil leaves
⅔ cup/150 ml olive oil
2 tomatoes
6½ tbsp/100 g butter
salt and pepper

Serves 4
Preparation time: 20 minutes
Cooking time: 35 minutes
Difficulty: ★ ★

2. Finely chop the shallots. Add the savory, chopped garlic, crushed coriander and basil leaves.

The noble sea bass, so imposing and prestigious, is an excellent match for the intensely aromatic herb savory. With an aroma like a mixture of mint and thyme, savory was called the "satyr's herb" by the Romans, who attributed great aphrodisiac properties to it. Imagine what such a charming union has in store for us!

The brill, a very virile fish, or the walleye, would superbly substitute for the bass in this dish. You can try either of these fish in making this recipe, or red mullet as well, which was our chef's original choice when he first created it. When slicing the fish, follow the grain of the flesh, from the head to the tail.

The chef recommends cooking the hollowed-out potatoes in a little water. This is essential if they are to remain in one piece without breaking apart.

Serve Scallops of Sea Bass with Savory very hot. The sauce and the potatoes can be reheated, but the fish must be served freshly cooked. This is a dish of quality that you will be proud to serve on important occasions.

Our wine expert suggests that you enjoy it with a Blanc de Blanc from Provence which, like savory, has a slight bite to it.

3. Add the olive oil to the garlic and herbs, salt lightly and sauté over low heat to make the sauce. Cook the potato "boats" in a little salted water. In another saucepan, boil the potato trimmings.

4. Skin, seed and chop the tomatoes. Cook them in a pan with a little oil until most of the moisture has evaporated. Purée the potato trimmings, and mix in the tomatoes. Adjust the seasoning if necessary, and put aside.

Sea Bass with Savory

5. Fillet the sea bass and cut into thin slices. Fry them in a pan with a little oil. Season with salt and pepper.

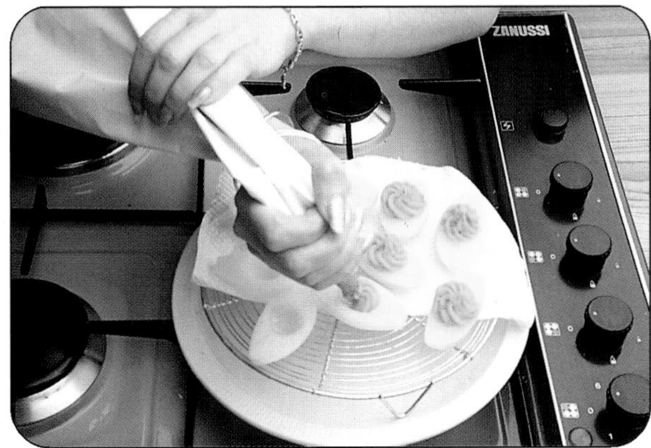

6. Use a pastry bag to garnish the potato boats with the potato and tomato purée. Cover the bottom of a serving platter with the shallot sauce. Place the fillets in it and surround them with the stuffed potatoes. Serve hot.

Walleye with

1. Fillet the fish (see basic recipe) and remove the skin. Cut the flesh into scallops. Cut the cauliflower into small florets, put them in a saucepan, and simmer them in the light cream. Salt lightly.

Ingredients:
1 walleye weighing
3 lbs 4 oz /1.5 kg
1 cauliflower
¾ cup/ 200 ml light cream
⅔ cup/150 ml oil
3½ tbsp/50 ml sherry
vinegar
2 tomatoes
3½ tbsp/50 ml porcini
juice
4 oz/115 g porcini
1 sweet red pepper
1 bunch of chives
1 truffle
6½ tbsp /100 ml heavy
cream
2 leaves of gelatin
1 tbsp butter
salt and pepper

Serves 4
Preparation time: 35 minutes
Cooking time: 30 minutes
Chilling time: 2 hours
Difficulty: ★ ★ ★

2. Make the porcini vinaigrette by mixing ⅔ of the oil, the sherry vinegar, salt, pepper, the skinned, seeded and chopped tomatoes, and the porcini juice. Whisk together and put aside. Mince the sweet pepper, chives and half of the truffle, and combine them.

The walleye is a relative newcomer to French cuisine, having been introduced to France as late as the 1950s. This large fish, which inhabits rivers, streams and lakes, is originally from central Europe and common in North America, and weighs up to 33 pounds (15 kg). Its exquisite white, firm flesh makes for a tender and delicious meal.
Porcini juice is an unusual ingredient available from gourmet stores or mail order companies. If the season is not right for fresh porcini, chanterelles or oyster mushrooms will also lend the dish a gentle woody flavor.
A tip from our chef: to ensure that the whipped cream does not turn liquid, make sure the cauliflower has cooled off completely after it is cooked.
The garnish is vital to this presentation, in which red, green and black are displayed against a white background. Lobster or lumpfish coral, which are bright red, could be used in place of sweet pepper, and the chives can be replaced with dill, which goes divinely with seafood. Black olive pieces could lend the touch of black; but on truly important occasions the precious truffle should not be left out. For a last touch of quality, put a thin layer of gelatin on top of the molds. When you turn them out they will shine like raw silk.
Our wine expert is of the opinion that the Sauvignon grape variety finds its best expression in the wines of the Baron de Ladoucette, and suggests his magnificent Pouilly-Fumé (Baron de L.).

3. Place a small spoonful of this mixture in the bottom of 4 small oval tart molds. Purée the cauliflower in a food processor as soon as it is tender.

4. Whip the heavy cream until stiff. When the cauliflower purée has thoroughly cooled, gently fold the whipped cream into it. Dissolve the leaves of gelatin in 3½ tbsp/ 50 ml water.

Porcini Vinaigrette

5. Add the gelatin to the cauliflower mixture and stir gently. Fill the tart molds with the mixture. Place in the refrigerator for 2 hours to set.

6. Salt and pepper the walleye fillets and fry them with a little oil and butter. Coat each plate with some porcini vinaigrette. Turn out a mold of cauliflower purée in the center of each plate. Place a very hot walleye scallop on each side of the purée, garnish with the remaining truffle, pepper and chives, and serve immediately.

Sole with

1. Peel the shallots and blanch them in 2 changes of water, then leave them to cool. Pour in the oil, add salt and pepper, and stew the shallots over low heat.

Ingredients:
1 sole weighing 2 lbs 10 oz/1.2 kg
3½ oz /100 g haddock
3½ oz /100 g whiting fillets
12 shallots
1 cup/250 ml oil
2 eggs
1¼ cups/300 ml crème fraîche
13 tbsp/200 g butter
⅔ cup/150 ml white wine
1 bunch chervil
½ sweet red pepper
salt and pepper

Serves 4
Preparation time: 35 minutes
Cooking time: 40 minutes
Difficulty: ★ ★

2. Cut the chilled haddock and whiting fillets into small pieces and place them in a food processor. Add the eggs, then blend the mixture well. Add salt, pepper and 6½ tbsp/100 ml of the crème fraîche. Blend again.

The Romans thought that the sole was shaped like the foot of Jupiter, the god of gods, the most powerful and prestigious of all. They would never have dared to think such a thing if the sole itself were not such a fine fish. Always highly regarded by the best chefs, it has been used in many delicious dishes. The one described here is yet another diamond in this collection. If you would like to make this recipe even more sumptuous, you can also make it with turbot.

To cook the sole to perfection, the skin, which is indigestible, should be removed. This is a difficult operation to perform, so do not hesitate to ask your fish retailer to do it.

Be careful not to add too much salt to the fish mousse, because the haddock will become saturated with it. Also, put the mousse through a sieve to remove the thin nerve strands; their presence would be detrimental to the elegance of the meal.

Serve Sole with Stewed Shallots very hot, accompanied by broccoli or zucchini, and steamed potatoes. Use small tartlet molds for the mousse. Their harmonious shape will lend the dish a last elegant touch. Simple but elegant, it will give your dinner parties a certain allure.

Our wine expert suggests a Puligny-Montrachet. This high quality white wine will delicately reconcile the sweetness of the shallots with the saltiness of the fish.

3. Use a card to press this mixture through a fine sieve to eliminate any small lumps of fish.

4. Grease the tartlet molds. Fill them with the mousse and place them in a double-boiler to cook for about 15 minutes.

Stewed Shallots

5. Clean the sole thoroughly and place it in a baking dish. Top with 1 tsp butter, sprinkle with salt and pepper, and pour in the white wine. Bake in a moderate oven for 15 minutes. Remove from the oven and sprinkle with the minced chervil. Add the rest of the crème fraîche and return to the oven for 10 minutes.

6. Remove the sole, and blend the cooking liquid well in a food processor. Adjust the seasoning and whip in the remaining butter. Cover a serving platter with this sauce. Arrange the sole and unmolded mousse on the platter, garnish with shallots, slivers of sweet pepper and chervil, and serve.

Sea Bass in

1. *Peel and chop the onions, celery root, leeks and carrots. Sauté the vegetables in a saucepan with half the butter.*

Ingredients:
1 sea bass,
3 lb 4½ oz /1.5 kg
3½ oz/100 g onions
1¾ oz/50 g celery root
3½ oz/100 g leeks without greens
3½ oz/100 g carrots
6½ tbsp/100 g butter
1 generous lb/500 g puff pastry (see basic recipe)
1 egg
salt and pepper

Serves 5
Preparation time: 40 minutes
Cooking time: 40 minutes
Difficulty: ★ ★ ★

2. *Fillet the sea bass (see basic recipe). Sprinkle the fillets with salt and pepper, coat with flour and fry briefly in a sauté pan with the remaining butter. Let the fillets cool before proceeding.*

The sea bass is called *loubine* on the Atlantic coast of France and *loup*, or "wolf," in Provence. Whatever name you give it, it is easily recognized: Sea bass has very few bones, and its flesh is smooth and firm, lean and delicate. It is caught mostly in the Mediterranean and has been prized since the time of the Romans.
Nonetheless, you can use a different sea fish when preparing this recipe, such as turbot or even pollack.
Our chef recommends cutting the leeks very thin, and to stop cooking the vegetables before they begin to brown. This is important, as they otherwise would risk drowning the taste of the fish. The accompaniment should enhance the taste of the bass, not overwhelm it.
This spring or autumn meal can be prepared the evening before and baked just before your guests arrive. Serve it hot. You can keep it hot for one hour after cooking by wrapping it in aluminum foil, which will retain all the moisture and flavor.
The pastry casing not only looks very impressive, it also preserves the mixture of flavors. If you wish to refine it further, serve the bass with a *beurre blanc* (see basic recipe), even with a touch of caviar added.
This festive dish has real class and is suitable for buffets or large gatherings.
Our wine expert suggests a Puligny-Montrachet Les Folatières, a superb white wine.

3. *When the vegetables are tender but not brown, leave them to cool. Roll out the puff pastry. Place a cooled bass fillet on it and cover with the vegetable mixture.*

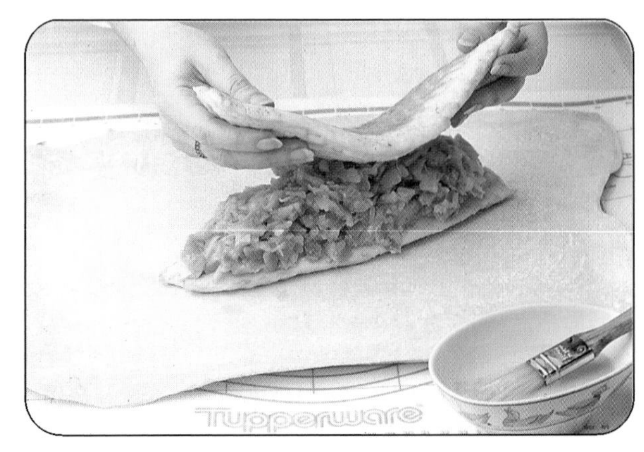

4. *Place the second fillet over the vegetables.*

Pastry Crust

5. Brush the whole fish and the puff pastry around it with beaten egg, then cover with a second layer of pastry and press to seal the edges.

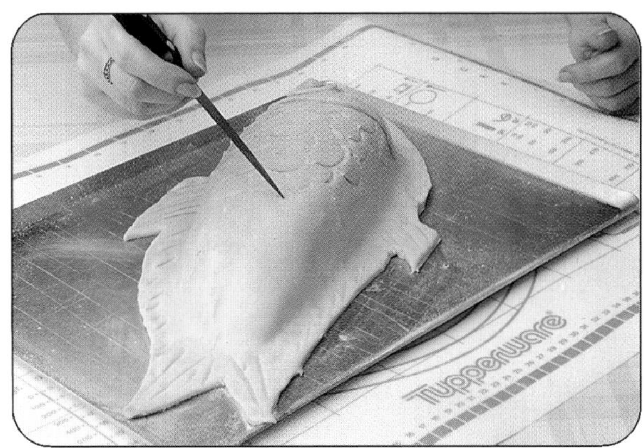

6. Cut the pastry into the shape of a fish and brush it with beaten egg. Etch scales into the pastry and cook in a hot oven for about 30 minutes.

Trout

1. *Use a knife to slit open the backs of the trout and remove their bones (see basic recipe).*

Ingredients:
4 trout, about
7 oz/200 g each
2 large slices
Bayonne ham
flour
1 sweet green pepper
1 sweet red pepper
6½ tbsp/100 ml oil
1 clove garlic
6½ tbsp/100 g butter
1 lemon
salt and pepper

Serves 4
Preparation time: 35 minutes
Cooking time: 20 minutes
Difficulty: ★ ★

2. *Cut the ham into strips and place them inside the trout. Add salt and pepper, then flour the fish.*

In the mountain streams of the Navarre region you can catch exquisite trout. They favor rushing streams, rivers and lakes, and are much sought after by anglers. This carnivorous fish, called *trôktês* (voracious) by the Greeks, has flavorful meat that is prized by gourmets. It is also rich in phosphorus, potassium and sulfur.

This is a recipe for an everyday meal that is out of the ordinary. As an alternative, the trout could be grilled instead of sautéed, but in either case, serve it straight after cooking so that you can enjoy the trout as fresh as possible. You can accompany this dish with risotto or boiled potatoes

Our chef, who is a master of his art, confided: "Cooking mobilizes our senses. You can only do it well if you feel. To succeed, you have to love; and in cooking, just as elsewhere, love obeys no laws..."

Our wine expert is of the opinion that a Pacherenc du Vic-Bilh, an undeservedly little-known wine from the banks of the Adour river, will be a magnificent accompaniment for a dish flavored with peppers.

3. *Wash the peppers thoroughly, remove the seeds and cut into thin strips.*

4. *Sauté the peppers in a saucepan with half of the oil. Add the chopped garlic at the end.*

à la Navarraise

5. Fry the trout in a pan with the remaining oil and some of the butter.

6. Arrange the trout on a serving platter. Sauté the peppers once more in the liquid left by the trout. Season with salt and pepper. Squeeze the lemon into the mixture, whisk in the rest of the butter, and pour this pepper sauce over the trout. Serve very hot.

Seafood

1. Peel and finely chop the onion and carrot. Peel the shallot and stick the cloves into it. Peel the garlic. Sauté the onion in a saucepan with a little butter. Add the carrot, shallot, garlic and bouquet garni. Cook, covered, over low heat.

Ingredients:
assorted seafood (fish, crustaceans, mussels etc.)
1 onion
1 carrot
1 shallot
3 whole cloves
3 cloves garlic
1 bouquet garni
8¾ oz/250 g navy beans
4 cups/1 liter fish stock (see basic recipe)
flour
salt and pepper

Serves 4
Preparation time: 20 minutes
Cooking time: 1 hour 30 minutes
Difficulty: ★

2. Add the navy beans, previously soaked in water, to this mixture.

This is a real fisherman's delight, with nothing left out!
Any seafood can be used in this recipe. Crowned by navy beans, this dish constitutes a valuable addition to *nouvelle cuisine*, an inexhaustible source of ideas. This is an original combination, full of charm, a savory *pièce de rèsistance* that will do honor to your table.
Use navy beans if they are available, and soak them in water for several hours before using them. Add fish stock or water as necessary while the beans are cooking, and adjust the seasoning halfway through the time.
Clean and trim the various kinds of seafood as appropriate before cooking it. Keep it hot on a plate covered with greased aluminum foil.
When the navy beans are cooked, arrange the seafood on top of them while they are still steaming hot. Sprinkle with finely chopped parsley and serve the Seafood Cassoulet very hot. Our wine expert suggests a Sancerre. Bon appètit!

3. Pour the fish stock over the navy beans, and add a little water. Cook over low heat.

4. Steam the mussels in a covered saucepan; they will cook in their own juice. Remove one shell from each and retain the rest.

Cassoulet

5. Cut the fish into small pieces.

6. Season and flour the seafood and fry it in a frying pan with the rest of the butter. When ready to serve, place the beans on the platter and top them with the seafood.

Red Mullet

1. Fillet the red mullet (see basic recipe), if necessary, and cut the bones into large pieces.

Ingredients:
2 large red mullet
1 carrot
1 onion
greens of 1 leek
2 vanilla beans
1 glass white wine
1 bouquet garni
¾ cup /200 ml
crème fraîche
7 tbsp/110 g butter
2 eggs
salt

Serves 4
Preparation time: 20 minutes
Cooking time: 20 minutes
Difficulty: ★★

2. Peel the carrot and onion and chop them, along with the leek greens. Slit open the vanilla beans, then use a sharp-tipped knife to remove the pulp and put it aside.

If you prefer light but healthy meals, nothing compares to the nutritional value of fish. Red mullet has particularly lean flesh, but is at the same time rich in protein, iodine, iron and phosphorus.
Vanilla, which is neither a spice nor a flavoring, but rather a perfume, will transfer its taste and aroma to the red mullet. Originally from the American tropics, vanilla has adapted very well to the hot and humid climate of Madagascar, which is where most of it is grown today.
Vanilla is a tonic and stimulant as well as being an aid to digestion. The subtle flavor of vanilla coupled with that of red mullet balances this very original dish perfectly.
To save time, ask your fish retailer to fillet the red mullet. There should be just a few bones left for you to remove. The best tool to use for this operation is a pair of tweezers. When adding the egg yolks to the sauce, whisk very vigorously to prevent them from cooking in the hot sauce. This recipe will require patience and concentration. Red mullet, which can be considered a sort of marine game, combines so well with vanilla that it may well become a favorite dish for formal occasions. Sumptuously aromatic, it will do honor to any important meal.
Our wine expert suggests a Muscadet.

3. Sauté the vegetables and fish bones in a saucepan with some butter. Add the white wine and bouquet garni. Cover with water, then season with salt. Add the vanilla beans and simmer for about 20 minutes over low heat.

4. Strain this mixture through a fine sieve, return to the heat and reduce the liquid by half. Stir in the crème fraîche and the vanilla pulp. Whisk vigorously and let thicken over low heat.

Fillets with Vanilla

5. Salt the red mullet fillets and fry them with a little oil.

6. Add the remaining butter to the sauce. When ready to serve, remove from heat and vigorously whisk in the egg yolks. Pour the sauce onto the serving platter. Arrange the red mullet fillets on it and serve hot.

Red Mullet

1. Gut and scale the red mullet. Soak the beef marrow in cold water. Peel and finely chop the shallots.

Ingredients:
4 red mullet
8 medallions of beef marrow
4 shallots
6½ tbsp/100 ml wine vinegar
½ bottle Chinon Rouge
4 tbsp crème fraîche
½ cup/120 g butter
1 tbsp olive oil
4 sprigs parsley
2 zucchini
salt and pepper

Serves 4
Preparation time: 20 minutes
Cooking time: 30 minutes
Difficulty: ★

2. Combine the shallots and wine vinegar in a saucepan and reduce until dry. Then add the Chinon and reduce again until the wine has completely evaporated. Stir in the crème fraîche.

Red mullet: What a feast! If you cannot obtain them, however, any other rock-dwelling fish may be substituted.

Very small, young rock mullet do not need to be gutted, which is why they are nicknamed "sea woodcock" in France. Do not remove the liver, a part of the fish highly regarded by gourmets. Red mullet is a fish with a high iodine content, so it should be cooked in a strongly-flavored oil like olive oil or hazelnut oil.

The choice of beef marrow is a calculated one; it combines well with the flavor of fish. It is possible to steam it, rather than poaching it, as well.

When adding the butter to the sauce, do not let it boil. It is best to keep the sauce just warm and whisk in small pieces of thoroughly chilled butter. A sauce made in this way is strongly flavored and very aromatic, and the Chinon adds a regional note. If you prefer less pronounced flavors, add more crème fraîche.

Beans or asparagus are a good addition to this delightful dish. Red Mullet in Beurre Rouge is a succulent combination subtly joining together different tastes, a festival of flavor that is sure to delight all culinary explorers.

It is customary to serve the same wine used in the sauce. However, our wine expert makes an exception in this case and suggests that a Bellet Rouge, a fine wine made in the Nice area, will enhance the marvelous regional mixture of this dish.

3. Continue to reduce for a few minutes over very low heat, then remove from the heat and gradually add small pieces of chilled butter. Season with a little salt and pepper.

4. Poach the marrow briefly in salted water.

in Beurre Rouge

5. Fry the red mullet in a pan with 1 tbsp each of butter and olive oil. Season with salt and pepper.

6. Trim the zucchini and poach in lightly salted water. Adjust the seasoning of the sauce. Coat the fish with it and serve hot, accompanied by the medallions of beef marrow, small sprigs of parsley and zucchini.

Red Mullet Fillets

1. Fillet the red mullet (see basic recipe). Cut up the bones and brown them in a frying pan with some oil. Peel the shallots, mushrooms and celery, cut them into small pieces, add to the bones and stir.

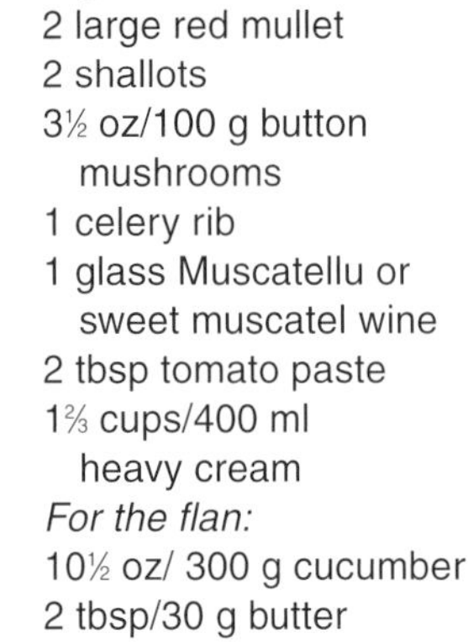

Ingredients:
2 large red mullet
2 shallots
3½ oz/100 g button mushrooms
1 celery rib
1 glass Muscatellu or sweet muscatel wine
2 tbsp tomato paste
1⅔ cups/400 ml heavy cream
For the flan:
10½ oz/ 300 g cucumber
2 tbsp/30 g butter
4 eggs
1⅔ cups/400 ml milk
1 pinch nutmeg
salt and pepper

Serves 4
Preparation time: 30 minutes
Cooking time: 1 hour
Difficulty: ★

2. When the vegetables are cooked, add the Muscatellu and the tomato paste. Season with a little salt and pepper, cover with water and simmer.

Muscatellu is the Corsican wine after which this recipe is named. A sweet muscatel wine, which is its equivalent in flavor can also be used. This stew is very obliging and incorporates everything, even the fish bones. If red mullet is not available, hogfish can be substituted for it.

This recipe is easy, if you follow our chef's advice. Sponge off the fillets with a paper towel before flouring them. The flour should not become moist or it will form a paste. In order to preserve their pink color, fry the fish flesh side down first, then turn onto the skin side just briefly. Our chef has chosen to use heavy cream for the sauce: It thickens during cooking, while thicker crème fraîche has the tendency to turn more liquid at the start. Let a little of the alcohol evaporate before adding the tomato paste. The flavor can be further enhanced by adding lemon juice.

Serve Red Mullet Fillets with Muscatellu hot. It can be reheated in the oven, but should be eaten the same day it is made.

Accompanied by a cucumber flan (also see basic recipe for vegetable flan), this simple and original dish will bring an exquisite elegance to a family meal.

Our wine expert suggests that you serve a dry white Sancerre wine.

3. Reduce the mixture to half its original volume. Add the cream and simmer gently for 2 or 3 minutes. Strain the sauce through a sieve and briefly bring to a boil.

4. For the flan, peel, seed and thinly slice the cucumbers and sauté them for 5 to 10 minutes in the butter. Season with salt and pepper.

with Muscatellu

5. Purée the cucumbers in a food processor, then turn into a bowl. Add the eggs, milk, salt, pepper, and a pinch of nutmeg. Whisk vigorously. Pour into greased ramekins and cook in a double boiler over medium heat for 20 minutes.

6. Flour the red mullet fillets, then fry them. Season with salt and pepper. Bring the sauce to a boil, whisking vigorously, and then pour it over the bottom of a serving platter. Arrange the red mullet fillets in the sauce and accompany with the cucumber flan.

Cap Corse

1. In a large pot, boil the lobsters in salted water for 10 minutes and then drain.

Ingredients:
4 small lobsters
6 tbsp oil
1 onion
1 celery rib
1 carrot
1 bouquet garni
1 bunch of chives
1 tbsp tomato paste
1 glass Cap Corse wine
2 cups/500 ml fish stock (see basic recipe)
1 pinch of saffron
¾ cup/200 ml heavy cream
3½ tbsp/50 g butter
salt and pepper

Serves 4
Preparation time: 1 hour
Cooking time: 45 minutes
Difficulty: ☆ ☆

2. Let them cool, then remove the flesh from the tails and claws.

The lobster, a marine crustacean that inhabits cold waters, has lean flesh rich in protein and mineral salts. It is the largest, tastiest and most sought-after of the crustaceans. The most highly regarded variety in French cuisine is the European lobster, which has a purplish-blue color, but Maine lobsters will taste equally exquisite when prepared according to this recipe.

When buying live lobster, check the reflexes of the eyes, feelers and pincers, and make sure there are no signs of combat injuries or mutilation.

After boiling the lobsters, remove the meat from the claws and tail and save the shells and body to make the sauce.

Adding wine to the sauce counteracts the acidity of the tomato sauce, and muscatel can be substituted for the "Cap Corse" used by our chef. The sauce is perfect when it sticks to a spoon. This simple dish can be kept for 24 hours and then reheated in a double boiler. Typically Corsican, and quite simply exquisite, our chef suggests serving it hot accompanied by an asparagus flan (see basic recipe for vegetable flan).

These lobsters will be a proud sight; their gastronomic majesty will give prestige to important occasions. Lobster obviously calls for the best white wine you have. Our wine expert suggests a Puligny-Montrachet.

3. Sauté all the lobster shells in a saucepan with the oil. Let the mixture catch slightly on the bottom of the pan.

4. Add the diced onion, celery and carrot, then the bouquet garni, chives and tomato paste. Stir and cook for 5 to 10 minutes.

Lobster

5. Add the wine, fish stock, 2 cups/500 ml water and the pinch of saffron. Season with salt and pepper and simmer until the liquid is reduced by a quarter.

6. Add the cream, stir and bring briefly to a boil. Strain the sauce through a fine sieve, whisk in the butter and pour over the sliced lobster. Serve accompanied by small asparagus flans.

Dog's Teeth Supreme

1. Fillet the dog's teeth and remove the skin (see basic recipe). Peel and finely chop the shallots. Grate the lime zest.

Ingredients:
4 dog's teeth fillets, about 6 oz/170 g
1 lime
4 lettuce leaves
fresh basil
1 bunch of lemon balm
2 shallots
3½ tbsp/50 g butter
1 glass dry white wine
2 cups/500 ml fish stock (see basic recipe)
2 cups/500 ml heavy cream
oven-proof plastic wrap
salt and pepper

Serves 4
Preparation time: 30 minutes
Cooking time: 20 minutes
Difficulty: ★ ★

2. Blanch the lettuce leaves in a saucepan full of lightly salted water for several seconds, then plunge them into iced water to halt the cooking process.

A close relative of the California sheepshead, and like it a saltwater fish, the dog's teeth has long teeth that gave it its name. Despite its fierce look and pointed teeth, it has firm and tasty flesh. It is moreover a large fish, sometimes reaching a length of almost a meter (3 feet). It is caught in the Mediterranean, particularly off the Corsican coast, where it likes to cruise from about April until the end of June.
Because it is a migratory fish, it is not available all year, but it can be replaced by tautog or California sheepshead. Ask your fish retailer to fillet the fish for you. It is a delicate operation and can be time-consuming.
You can begin cooking the fish in an oven-proof frying pan. After the liquid has come to a boil, cover the pan before putting it in the oven. Add butter to the sauce to tone down the acidity that sometimes comes from white wine.
Dog's Teeth Supreme with Lemon Balm is easy to make, and our chef likes to serve it hot accompanied by a shallot flan (see basic recipe for vegetable flan). This everyday dish transforms ordinary ingredients by giving you the chance to discover combinations of flavors: the slight tartness of lemon balm, the sweetness of the shallot, and the delicately firm consistency of the fish.
Dishes based on exotic aromas need fine white wines. Our wine expert proposes an Alsatian Tokay (Pinot Gris).

3. Place a basil leaf on each fillet. Sprinkle with salt, pepper and some lime zest. Wrap the fillets in a green lettuce leaf, then in oven-proof plastic wrap.

4. Finely chop the lemon balm and shallots. Thoroughly grease a baking dish with the butter and sprinkle in the shallots. Place the fillets in the dish and cover them with lemon balm.

with Lemon Balm

5. Pour the white wine and fish stock over the fillets. Add a little salt and pepper and bake for about 10 minutes in a hot oven.

6. Remove the fish rolls and keep them hot. Reduce the cooking liquid to ¼ its initial volume. Add the cream and continue to reduce. Season with salt and pepper and strain the sauce through a fine sieve. Remove the plastic wrap from the fish rolls, and serve accompanied by the sauce and small vegetable flans.

Cod with

1. *Peel and finely chop the shallots; set them aside. Chop the avocado.*

Ingredients:
1 cod fillet,
 1 lb 11 oz/800 g
2 shallots
1 avocado
4 heads of chicory
4 tomatoes
6½ tbsp/100 ml white wine
1 cup/250 ml heavy cream
⅓ cup/80 g butter
salt and pepper

Serves 4
Preparation time: 30 minutes
Cooking time: 30 minutes
Difficulty: ★

2. *Clean the chicory thoroughly, then cut it into julienne. Cut the tomatoes into thin half-circles.*

Generally, the cod is a large saltwater fish measuring up to one and a half meters (almost 4 ft) in length. It is normally cut into fillets, steaks or slices. For this recipe you should use fillets, and fillets of just about any fish can be prepared in this way. Take care when cooking them, as cod breaks apart particularly easily when overcooked. Our chef advises you to grill the dish briefly after removing it from the oven to brown the avocados and tomatoes slightly.
Broccoli or asparagus can replace the chicory without changing the flavor of this dish adversely. Serve it hot. If there is some left over, it can be served cold at the next meal, without sauce, and accompanied by a mixed salad.
The cod and chicory contain a perfect balance of protein and vitamins. Avocado is relatively high in calories, but is nonetheless an excellent food because of its high concentrations of vitamins A, B1, B2, B6, C and E.
Our wine expert recommends a Bandol Blanc (Ott Domaine). The delicate flesh of the fish and the oiliness of the avocado is a combination that suits the vigor and tenderness of this white wine.

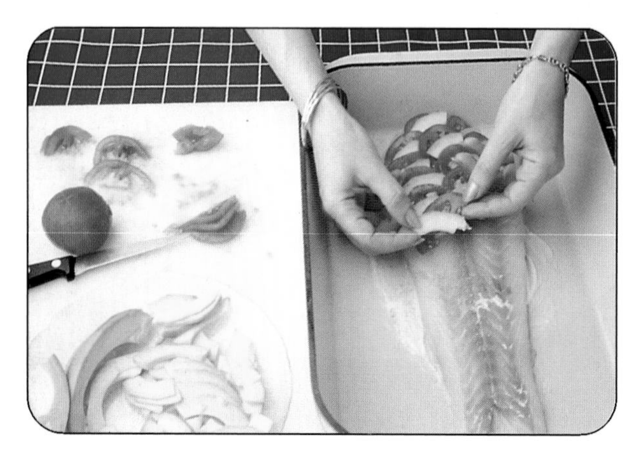

3. *Grease a baking dish and place the cod fillet in it. Sprinkle with salt and pepper, then arrange the pieces of tomato and avocado to resemble scales on the fish.*

4. *Sprinkle shallots over the bottom of the baking dish, pour in the white wine and bake in a medium oven for about 20 minutes.*

Avocado

5. While the fish is cooking, melt half the butter in a saucepan. Add salt and pepper to the chicory and simmer in the butter with the lid on. Leave the chicory slightly crisp.

6. Arrange the cod fillet on a serving platter. Reduce the cooking liquid by half, then add the cream to it and boil briefly. Adjust the seasoning, whip in the rest of the butter, bring briefly to a boil, strain through a fine sieve and serve as accompaniment to the cod.

Streaked Weever and

1. *Fillet the weever (see basic recipe), remove the skin, and cut each fillet in half.*

Ingredients:
1 streaked weever, 2 lbs 10 oz/1.2 kg
1 shallot
3½ tbsp/50 g butter
1¼ cups/300 ml white wine
1 bouquet garni
4 cups/1 liter mussels
1 orange
3 cups/750 ml heavy cream
1 pinch of saffron

Serves 4
Preparation time: 30 minutes
Cooking time: 20 minutes
Difficulty: ★

2. *Peel and mince the shallots, and sauté them in a saucepan with a little butter.*

The streaked weever, a saltwater fish, has the peculiarity of often living buried under the sand. Although the quality of its flesh is highly regarded, it is feared because of its venomous spines. Before cooking the fish, you need to don a pair of gloves and removes these spines, as well as the fins. It would be a good idea to let a fish retailer prepare it; they have experience dealing with these tasks.
The streaked weever cooks quickly, 5 to 6 minutes maximum, so be careful not leave it in the mussel stock too long.
Depending on your preference, you can also make this dish with other shellfish.
As in bouillabaisse, small croutons spread with garlic purée will form a marvelous accompaniment to the weever fillets. Finely chopped fennel also goes very well with it, and both of them together would be even better.
This recipe is a regional one, but streaked weever is available at good fish markets. Rich in iodine and calcium, it is ideal for convalescents.
Our wine expert suggests an Alsatian Tokay (Pinot Gris), which marvelously highlights the royal flavor of saffron.

3. *Add the white wine, bouquet garni and mussels. Cover the saucepan and steam the mussels until they open. Remove the mussels from their shells and put them aside.*

4. *Peel the orange and cut the zest into thin strips. Blanch these, changing the water 3 or 4 times.*

Mussels in Saffron Cream

5. Strain the liquid in which the mussels were cooked through a fine sieve. Pour it onto the weever fillets and poach them for 4-6 minutes.

6. When cooked, remove the weever fillets from the pan. Add the cream and saffron and simmer the sauce until it thickens. Whisk the remaining butter into the sauce, and pour over the weever fillets. Garnish with the mussels, orange zest and strands of saffron.

Carp Turnovers

1. *Fillet the carp (see basic recipe) and cut 4 generous, thin slices from the best part. Cut the rest of the flesh into pieces.*

Ingredients:
1 carp, 3 lbs 4 oz/ 1.5 kg
3 egg yolks
6½ tbsp/100 ml crème fraîche
10½ oz/300 g carrots
1 bunch of small onions
1 tbsp sugar
3 shallots
2 cups/500 ml Bourgueil
3½ tbsp/50 g butter
salt and pepper

Serves 4
Preparation time: 30 minutes
Cooking time: 25 minutes
Difficulty: ★★

2. *Put aside the slices of fish and purée the rest. Add the egg yolks, salt and pepper, and crème fraîche. Purée again until absolutely smooth.*

This recipe will send delightful fragrances through your house on an autumn evening... In the area our chef comes from, ponds full of carp abound, and he has concocted this delicious regional dish as an homage to his home. One might be able to find live carp at the fish retailer: There is no better guarantee of freshness. Flatten the carp scallops well to prevent them from curling up during cooking.
If you wish, you can decorate the serving platter with a few chanterelles. Lemon juice will prevent them from turning black and help keep their lovely yellow-orange color. White wine could be used instead of red in the sauce; either one will complement this carp dish.
Serve Carp Turnovers with Bourgueil hot, accompanied by small vegetables. We have chosen pearl onions and carrots, but asparagus would also be excellent. This dish can be reheated and keeps for two or three days in the refrigerator.
The red wines of Bourgueil are known for their intense fruitiness, and it is this quality that makes it so perfectly suited to this recipe. Our wine expert suggests a Bourgueil (Domaine Paul Maître). With its raspberry bouquet, this magnificent wine is one of the best in its price range.

3. *Place about 2 heaped tablespoons of this filling on each fillet. Fold them over and use toothpicks or oven-proof plastic wrap to keep them closed.*

4. *Peel and trim some of the carrots; peel the onions. Place the carrots and onions in separate saucepans, cover with water and add a little butter to each. Sprinkle with the sugar and simmer. When the water has evaporated, the vegetables will be slightly glazed.*

with Bourgueil

5. Peel the shallots and remaining carrots, and dice them. Place them in a baking dish along with the carp turnovers. Add the carp bones, pour in the red wine and place in the oven to cook for about 20 minutes.

6. Place the fish turnovers on a serving platter. Remove the bones from the baking dish and purée the remaining sauce. On the stovetop, reduce it by half and then whisk in rest of the butter. Pour the sauce over the turnovers and serve with the glazed carrots and onions.

Cod Flakes with

1. Peel the potatoes and cut them into thin slices. Peel and slice the onions.

Ingredients:
2 lb 6 oz/1.2 kg salted cod
2 lb 3 oz/1 kg potatoes
14 oz/400 g large onions
3 carrots
1 leek
⅔ cup/150 ml oil
7 oz/200 g *trompette de la morte* mushrooms
1 bunch flat-leaf parsley
salt and pepper

Serves 6
Preparation time: 40 minutes
Cooking time: 25 minutes
Difficulty: ★ ★

2. Peel the carrots and the leek and cut them into a fine julienne.

Cod, an inhabitant of cold waters, is often sold salted and sometimes dried as well. You will therefore have to start by soaking it in cold water for 12 hours or overnight to remove the salt. To do this most effectively, place it in the water with the skin facing upwards. If possible, do not let the fish touch the bottom of the container. After it has soaked, skin the cod, remove its bones, and break the flesh into flakes. This is a simple operation.

Salted cod has a higher energy value than unsalted cod, and many other qualities to recommend it, as well. It has always been highly regarded. A staple food for meatless days, it also had strategic uses, making it possible for people to hold out for a long time during a siege without fresh rations.

In this recipe the cod is accompanied by the most popular vegetable of all, the potato. Do not take the risk of tossing the potato galette like a pancake, but turn it gently. Cod Flakes with Potato Galette will give everyday meals a special touch.

Muscadet sur lie is France's most maritime wine. Our wine expert assures us that it is the best possible companion for this ocean-going fish.

3. In a frying pan with a little oil sauté the onions. In another frying pan, sauté the trompette de la morte mushrooms. Season with salt and pepper.

4. Place a pan with oil over heat. Cover the bottom of it with overlapping slices of potato to form a galette. Cook like a pancake.

Potato Galette

5. Place the sautéed onions on the potato galette. Spread them evenly and cover with another galette of overlapping potato slices. Turn the galette so that it can brown on both sides.

6. Poach the cod, previously soaked to remove the salt. Break it up into flakes. Place the potato galette on a serving platter. Arrange the cod flakes, julienned vegetables and trompette de la morte mushrooms around it, garnish with parsley, and serve.

Turbot with

1. Peel and finely chop the ginger and garlic. Finely dice the red pepper and grate the lime zest.

Ingredients:
1 turbot weighing 2 lb 6 oz/1.2 kg
1 piece of ginger
2 cloves of garlic
1 sweet red pepper
1 tbsp butter
1⅔ cups/400 ml fish stock (see basic recipe)
¾ cup/150 g wild rice
12 canned baby corn
6½ tbsp /100 ml crème fraîche
1 lime
1 bunch of Thai basil
salt and pepper.

Serves 4
Preparation time: 20 minutes
Cooking time: 40 minutes
Difficulty: ★

2. In a frying pan, let the garlic and ginger sweat in the butter without browning. Add the sweet red pepper and mix everything together with the fish stock. Simmer for 1 minute.

The name of this recipe alone is enough to evoke thoughts of marvelous voyages. To give this turbot an exotic touch, visit one of the ever more numerous shops supplying Asian spices. There you will find the baby corn and the unusual Thai basil.

It is important to cook the turbot gently. Simply keeping the stock at a simmer is enough, as the flesh breaks up if cooked too brusquely. To prevent the wild rice from falling apart, it should be steamed, if possible. Do not forget to rinse it in cold water after cooking: If it cools off in the air, wild rice forms a sticky paste.

If desired, angler fish can replace the turbot. Its flesh is just as refined and will maintain the exceptional quality of this recipe.

The delicate whiteness of the turbot combined with the somber brilliance of wild rice will provide an extraordinary contrast worthy of the completely original flavor of this recipe. Turbot with Thai Basil is worth saving for friends you particularly want to spoil.

Our wine expert suggests a Vouvray Moelleux (Domaine G. Huet). This wine will lead you to the discovery that the floating markets of Bangkok have something in common with those on the peaceful banks of the Loire.

3. Soak the rice overnight and cook it in salted water. Poach the baby corn.

4. Add salt and pepper to the fish stock. Make four fillets from the turbot, and then cut them in slices perpendicular to the backbone. Place the turbot in the stock and simmer 2 minutes on each side.

Thai Basil

5. Remove the turbot from the liquid and keep it hot. Reduce the stock by half, then add the crème fraîche.

6. Shred the Thai basil leaves and add them to the sauce. Blanch the grated lime zest and add it as well. Cover and simmer for a few minutes. Pour the sauce over the turbot fillets and serve accompanied by the rice and the corn.

Walleye Roulades

1. Fillet the walleye and cut 4 large pieces. Put the rest of the fish in the freezer to chill. Make a fish stock (see basic recipe) out of the bones, shallots, carrot, leek and white wine.

Ingredients:
1 walleye
3 shallots
1 carrot
white of 1 leek
¾ cup/200 ml white wine
1 egg
¾ cup/200 ml crème fraîche
chives
3½ oz/100 g flat-leaf parsley
salt and pepper

Serves 4
Preparation time: 25 minutes
Cooking time: 20 minutes
Difficulty: ★ ★

2. Place the chilled walleye flesh (about 6⅓ oz/180 g) in a food processor. Add the egg, salt and pepper, and blend. Finely chop the chives.

This recipe has a regional touch due to the use of walleye, a fish that inhabits streams and lakes, which is much prized in the Forrez. If it is difficult to obtain—it only appears in shops in the fall—there is no reason to wait until autumn to enjoy this dish: Any other fish with white, firm flesh will do just as well. Our chefs' recipes thrive on travel and changes of venue.

It has been said of parsley that it is one of the most precious health foods nature has generously put at the disposal of the human race. Its many properties include being a general stimulant and nerve tonic.

The walleye flesh for the stuffing must be frozen before you made the fish purée. Do not grill the fish bones to make the stock, as this could make it cloudy. Reduce the fish stock well before adding the crème fraîche: The quality of the sauce depends on this.

Prick the roulades with a needle so that they do not burst while cooking. Walleye should be served hot and not reheated. On the other hand, if you have leftover roulades, they can be enjoyed cold, in a salad. Served hot, they are delicious with spinach sautéed in butter. The originality of these delicious little rolls will enchant your guests and confirm the reputation of your cooking.

The Sauvignon wines grown on the hills of Sancerre are remarkable. Serve the Sancerre (Domaine H. Bourgeois) lightly chilled, at 55 °F/12 °C.

3. Blend half of the crème fraîche into this mixture. When the fish purée has become smooth, add the chives. Mix again briefly.

4. Lay out the walleye fillets and place 1 heaping tbsp of the fish purée in the center of each, then roll them up. Wrap in ovenproof plastic wrap and tie the ends.

with Parsley

5. When the fish stock is ready, strain it through a fine sieve and reduce by half. Add the rest of the crème fraîche and let the sauce thicken over gentle heat. Adjust the seasoning if necessary. Remove 6½ tbsp/100 ml of the fish sauce, let it cool, and blend with the parsley. Set aside.

6. Poach the walleye roulades for 10 minutes. When ready to serve, add the hot sauce to the parsley mixture. Whisk the sauce and pour it onto a serving platter. Cut the rolls through diagonally, arrange them on the platter and serve hot.

Fish Stew

1. Peel and chop the shallots. Finely chop the celery root. Peel the carrots, shape them as shown and slice them into rounds.

Ingredients:
1 quart/1 liter mussels
1 sole
1 salmon
4 mussels
3 shallots
3½ oz/100 g celery root
2 carrots
1 cup/250 ml white wine
thyme
bay leaf
2 star anise
4 scallops
½ bunch of chives
½ bunch of chervil
salt
peppercorns

Serves 4
Preparation time: 35 minutes
Cooking time: 30 minutes
Difficulty: ☆ ☆

The flavor of star anise combines marvelously with fish. This simple recipe is subtle in taste, and gives the impression of being very elaborate despite its simplicity. You will be admired for your *savoir-faire*, and no one needs to know that this sophisticated dish is actually very easy to prepare.

The chef advises to make sure the vegetables stay crisp. This is essential to the perfection this aromatic dish demands.

Remember that the salmon should keep its pink color if it is not to be too dry. If you wish to vary the fish used, do not lose salmon's beautiful color. Red mullet can be used instead, but leave on the skin.

You can add the liquid left after cooking the mussels to the broth; this will give it more flavor. Consume Fish Stew with Star Anise right away, with enjoyment, and discover a complex wine with mineral aromas: an Alsatian Tokay (Pinot Gris).

2. In a saucepan containing half the wine, steam the mussels over high heat for 2-3 minutes or just until the mussels open.

3. Fillet the sole and salmon and cut the flesh into strips. Put aside.

4. Pour a little water and the rest of the white wine into a saucepan and add the vegetables and herbs: shallots, carrots, celery root, thyme, bay leaf and star anise. Add salt and peppercorns, and simmer over gentle heat.

with Star Anise

5. When this broth is finished, strain half of the liquid through a sieve into an ovenproof pan containing the strips of fish and the scallops, and bake in the oven for 10 minutes.

6. Whisk the butter into the rest of the broth. Adjust the seasoning and pour over the salmon, sole, scallops and shelled mussels. Garnish with chives and chervil.

Red Mullet

1. Remove the bones from the red mullet without detaching the fillets from the head and tail (see basic recipe). Salt and pepper the open side, then lay the fish flat with the open side down.

Ingredients:
4 red mullet, each 5¼ oz/150 g
3½ tbsp/50 g butter
¾ cup/200 ml heavy cream
3 limes
1 bunch of dill
salt and pepper

Serves 4
Preparation time: 40 minutes
Cooking time: 20 minutes
Difficulty: ✶

2. Fry the red mullet in a pan with the butter, but only on one side.

The red mullet, prized since ancient times, is a medium-sized fish with lean flesh that is rich in protein, iodine, iron, phosphorus and vitamin C.
In France it is caught primarily in Vendée and the Cherbourg region, and can be obtained from February through June. It is also imported from Senegal, which means that you may be able to buy it as early as October.
An infallible sign of freshness is if the fish have retained their red or pink color. If this has grown dim, the fish has begun to deteriorate. The flesh should be firm, the body almost rigid, the skin taut and the eyes protruding and clear. The red mullet is a delicate fish, and should be eaten very soon after purchase. It can be replaced by cunner or bream.
Red mullet contains quite a bit of iodine and combines well with all sauces, sweet and sour. The sauce and fish can be reheated separately. If well prepared, this small fish takes on larger dimensions and will be a joy to all at your table.
In the opinion of our wine expert, Provence must have the honor in the case of red mullet. Serve a Bandol Blanc.

3. In a saucepan, bring the heavy cream to a boil while whisking occasionally.

4. Add the juice from 2 of the limes and return to a boil.

with Lime

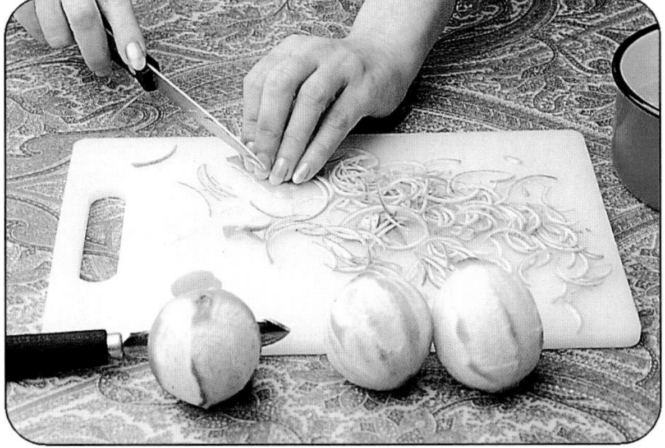

5. When the cream sauce is reduced, add a little salt and pepper, then return to a boil for a few minutes. Cut the lime zest into thin strips and blanch them.

6. Pour the lime sauce over the plate, and then place the red mullet in it. Strew with lime zest and some sprigs of dill.

Cod à la

1. Peel the onions and carrots. Clean the leeks and celery, and chop all the vegetables. Sauté them in a frying pan with half of the olive oil.

Ingredients:
1 lb 14 oz/800 g salted cod fillet
2 onions
2 carrots
1 rib of celery
white of 1 leek
6½ tbsp/100 ml olive oil
4 fresh tomatoes
1 bouquet garni
1 tbsp tomato paste
4 cloves of garlic
1 whole clove
1 glass dry white wine
1¾ oz/50 g black olives
1 tbsp capers
2 gherkins
1 pinch of saffron
1 tbsp mustard
salt and pepper

Serves 4
Preparation time: 20 minutes
Cooking time: 35 minutes
Difficulty: ★

This recipe will give you an opportunity to discover a delightful dish that has been long neglected: A variation of bouillabaisse made with cod that is extremely simple to make. Fans of Provençal cuisine know this ragoût well, one that is still faithfully prepared in the Mediterranean region. Pickled pork and a poached egg can be added, both of which go perfectly with the flavor medley of capers, mustard, gherkins and saffron.

Our chef advises thoroughly soaking the cod in water to remove the salt. Be sure that the fish you choose has firm white flesh. Serve it very hot. Like all ragoûts, it can easily be reheated. This flavorful dish will put a little sunlight into family meals.

The iodized aroma of a Bandol Blanc will go magnificently with the splendor of Cod à la Provençal.

2. Skin, seed and dice the tomatoes. Add them to the vegetables along with the bouquet garni. Add salt, pepper and the tomato paste.

3. Put in the peeled cloves of garlic and the clove, and pour in the white wine. Simmer over gentle heat. Add a little water if necessary.

4. Mix in the black olives, capers and the gherkins, cut into round slices.

Provençal

5. Season the bouillabaisse with the saffron and mustard, and mix well. Continue to cook for a while, then set aside.

6. Slice the soaked and drained cod fillets and fry them in a pan with the rest of the oil for several minutes. Finish cooking them in the bouillabaisse. Serve hot accompanied by potatoes.

Scallops of Sea Bass

1. *Scale and fillet the sea bass, then halve the fillets. Peel and slice the onion. Grease the bottom of a baking dish. Sprinkle in the sliced onion and place the fish fillets on top.*

Ingredients:
1 sea bass, 2 lb 6 oz/1.2 kg
1 onion
6½ tbsp/100 ml olive oil
2 shallots
4 pieces bone marrow
6½ tbsp/100 ml red wine vinegar
6½ tbsp/100 ml fish stock (see basic recipe) or 1 fish bouillon cube
6½ tbsp/100 ml crème fraîche
6½ tbsp/100 g butter
1 pinch of coarse salt
salt and pepper

Serves 4
Preparation time: 25 minutes
Cooking time: 25 minutes
Difficulty: ★★

The sea bass is a fish with prestige, prized for the delicacy of its flesh since Roman times. A gastronomic delight, it is also a healthy food: Like all saltwater fish, it is rich in iodine, a trace element that plays an important role in the growth process. It is also a source of phosphorus and of the B-complex vitamins and vitamin D.

Hake, which is easier to obtain than sea bass, also works very well with this recipe. The chef recommends making some incisions in the fish to prevent the fillets from shrinking during cooking.

Marrow needs to be well seasoned, so be sure to sprinkle it with salt and pepper while it is cooking. Some grains of coarse salt added at the last moment will subtly bring out its luscious flavor. To make the sauce smoother, blend it in a food processor before serving. Serve the bass scallops hot with small young peas; they will enhance this dish with their fresh and lively appearance.

Particularly recommended for children because of its health-giving properties, this meal will delight the whole family.

The succulent flesh of the bass and the tender taste of the marrow deserve a fine white Burgundy. Our wine expert suggests a Meursault Genevrières.

2. *Pour the olive oil over the bass fillets and top each with a small piece of butter. Season with salt and pepper.*

3. *Peel and finely chop the shallots. Cut the marrow into round slices.*

4. *Pour the wine vinegar into a saucepan. Add the shallots and reduce until the vinegar has evaporated.*

with Bone Marrow

5. Add the fish stock, or a bouillon cube dissolved in the same amount of water, and reduce by half. Stir in the crème fraîche and let the sauce thicken. Fry the pieces of bone marrow in a frying pan with a little butter.

6. Whisk the rest of the butter into the sauce and strain through a fine sieve. Bake the fish fillets in a hot oven for 15 minutes. Cover the bottom of a platter with the sauce and arrange the bass fillets on the platter. Place the round pieces of marrow on the fish, sprinkle with a little coarse salt and serve.

Haddock Supreme

1. Clean the Brussels sprouts. Bring salted water to a boil in a saucepan and cook the sprouts, making sure they stay slightly crisp.

Ingredients:
1 lb 14 oz/800 g haddock
14 oz/400 g Brussels sprouts
2 cups/500 ml milk
thyme
bay leaf
parsley
3½ oz/100 g shallots
⅔ cup/150 ml white wine
6½ tbsp/100 ml vinegar
2 tbsp/30 ml crème fraîche
13 tbsp/200 g butter
salt and pepper

Serves 4
Preparation time: 10 minutes
Cooking time: 30 minutes
Difficulty: ☆

2. Pour the milk into a large pan. Add the thyme, bay leaf and parsley. Cut the haddock into portions and poach it in the milk.

It is said that the well-known Brussels sprout—which is mainly grown in the northern part of France—was imported to Belgium by the Roman legions, that is, that they are of Italian origin.
Most people are quite familiar with these miniature cabbages, but usually only cook them whole. In this recipe you will discover that they are more easily digestible, and better able to absorb the flavorings used in their preparation, when chopped before cooking. They will seem even more succulent than usual. Brussels sprouts are generally available from September through March. Choose ones that are green and firm. The best ones are those picked before the first frosts. As they are suitable for freezing, you can even put in a supply. They are rich in sulfur, potassium and vitamins. Eat them often, as they have few calories and are excellent as part of a balanced diet.
Traditionally, Brussels sprouts are served with meat. The originality of this recipe consists in combining them with fish.
You will not meet with any difficulties while making this dish; you will only have the pleasure of preparing something that is easy to make and the joy of new flavors.
Haddock Supreme with Brussels Sprouts will add a sumptuous note to everyday meals. Our wine expert suggests a Gros Plant from Nantes.

3. Peel and finely chop the shallots. Place them in a saucepan and pour in the white wine and vinegar.

4. Reduce the liquid by ¾, then add the crème fraîche. Chop up half of the Brussels sprouts, sauté them slightly in butter and put them aside.

with Brussels Sprouts

5. Reduce the sauce by half, then whisk in the butter. Season with a little salt and pepper.

6. Drain the haddock fillets. Arrange them on the serving platter with the chopped Brussels sprouts in the middle. Decorate with some whole sprouts. Pour over the sauce and serve hot.

Whiting

1. *Remove the backbones of the fish by cutting them open along their backs (see basic recipe).*

Ingredients:
2 whiting
1 cup plus 3 tbsp/150 g bread crumbs
6½ tbsp/100 ml white Cassis
1 bunch of basil
¾ cup/200 ml fish stock (see basic recipe)
13 tbsp/200 g butter
1 lemon
salt and pepper

Serves 2
Preparation time: 35 minutes
Cooking time: 25 minutes
Difficulty: ★

2. *Place the whiting in a greased baking dish, season with salt and pepper, and sprinkle generously with the breadcrumbs.*

In Provence, this dish is often made with the forked hake, a small fish native to the Mediterranean with lean, delicate flesh. It is highly regarded locally, but does not transport well.

The whiting is a relative of the haddock and the cod, and it inhabits the Atlantic, where it can be caught from Norway to Spain. It can be obtained nearly all year round at an affordable price. Its flesh is just as delicate as that of the forked hake, but flaky, and it falls apart easily during cooking. Be careful not to let it break apart at the last moment when placing it on the serving plates.

The sauce must be cooked over low heat to prevent the butter from curdling. Serve Whiting with Basil hot, with spinach or broccoli. *Bon appètit*; and be sure to eat it all up, as it cannot be reheated.

Our wine expert recommends a Cassis Blanc, an excellent marriage of noble products from the same region.

3. *Top the fish with several small pieces of butter and carefully pour in the wine. Bake the fish for 10 minutes in a moderate oven.*

4. *Wash the basil, pluck the leaves and mince them.*

with Basil

5. Arrange the whiting on a serving platter. Pour the cooking liquid into a saucepan and add the fish stock. Reduce by ¾, then whisk in the remaining butter.

6. Add the chopped basil and lemon juice to the sauce and whisk vigorously. Adjust the seasoning and serve the whiting accompanied by the basil sauce.

Plaice with Mussels

1. Fillet and skin the plaice. Finely chop the shallots, spread them over the bottom of a greased baking dish, and place the plaice fillets in it.

Ingredients:
4 plaice fillets
2 cups/½ liter cultivated mussels
4 shallots
2 sprigs of parsley
7 oz/200 g horn of plenty mushrooms, chopped
2 cups/500 ml dry white wine
¾ cup/200 ml crème fraîche
10 tbsp/150 g butter
1¾ oz/50 g dried horn of plenty mushrooms
juice of 1 lemon
salt and pepper

Serves 4
Preparation time: 25 minutes
Cooking time: 20 minutes
Difficulty: ★

2. Chop the parsley and mushrooms and sprinkle them over the fish.

In traditional paintings, the horn of plenty, or cornucopia, is a symbol for abundance and endless wealth. Here, it is the name of a little gray mushroom, also known as *trompette de la morte* ("trumpet of death") or black chanterelle. Our chef could not resist this poetic touch in the title, as the flavorful mushrooms create a subtle and beneficent aroma in combination with the mussels.

The plaice is a diamond-shaped flatfish caught mainly in the Atlantic, the English Channel and the North Sea; it is very seldom found in the Mediterranean. It can be replaced by with other fishes with white flesh, for example the cunner or the John Dory are ideally suited. Pay careful attention to the cooking time, as the flesh should remain firm. If cooked too long, the fish will disintegrate.

Mussels are cultivated using ropes hung into the water. Wash them thoroughly and patiently to get rid of the sand they often contain. This recipe could also be made with clams or scallops, which are both delicious as well.

For shipboard meals or dinners "on the run," Plaice with Mussels and Horns of Plenty will arouse the appetite and, with its open-air aromas, make you dream of new horizons and the rising sun.

Our wine expert suggests a white wine: a Gros Plant from Nantes.

3. Pour the white wine and a glass of water into the baking dish, add salt and pepper, and bake in a moderate oven for 10 minutes.

4. Strain the cooking liquid from the baking dish into a saucepan containing the mussels and add the lemon juice. Reduce for 2-3 minutes.

and Horns of Plenty

5. Stir in the crème fraîche, blend gently and continue to reduce over low heat.

6. Add butter to this sauce while stirring gently. Arrange the plaice fillets on a serving platter. Pour the sauce over the bottom of the platter together with the mussels, garnish with the dried horn of plenty mushrooms, and grate some pepper onto each fillet. Serve hot.

Brill with

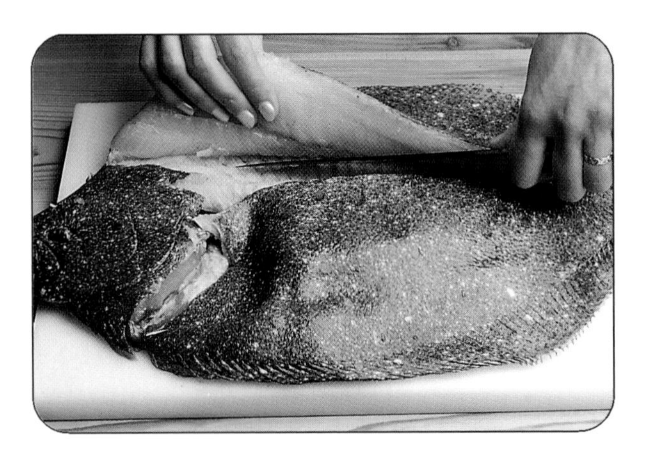

1. *Fillet the brill and remove its skin (see basic recipe).*

Ingredients:
1 brill, 2 lb 6 oz/1.2 kg
1 leek
1 carrot
3½ oz/100 g button mushrooms
1 rib of celery
3½ oz/100 g green string beans
1 shallot
6½ tbsp/100 ml fish stock (see basic recipe)
1 glass Noilly vermouth
pinch of saffron
6½ tbsp/100 ml crème fraîche
1 lemon
salt and pepper

Serves 5
Preparation time: 40 minutes
Cooking time: 30 minutes
Difficulty: ★

2. *Open each fillet in the middle and sprinkle lightly with salt and pepper.*

Here is an original recipe specially created by our chef using brill, a seawater fish caught on the Atlantic coast of France that can be obtained all year round. Its flesh tends to fall apart, so handle it with care.
The brill could easily be replaced with turbot. Novices have difficulty in differentiating between the brill and the turbot, which are extremely similar. Run your finger along the brown part of the skin. The brill is smooth and glossy, while the turbot has a grainy skin texture. Take a good look at the fish: If its eyes are bright and shiny and its gills are bright red, it is fresh.
To retain the freshness of the the lemon juice, the chef recommends adding it at the last moment and not letting the sauce boil again afterward.
As to the vegetables, choose ones with good color but above all ones that are firm and crispy. The originality and gastronomic pleasure of this dish derive from the crispness of the vegetables. They can be poached or steamed; either way they will keep their flavor and crunch merrily on the teeth.
For a fine ocean-going fish, a fine white Burgundy is ideal, says our wine expert. He suggests a Meursault Charmes.

3. *Cut the leeks, carrots, mushrooms and celery into a fine julienne.*

4. *Poach of steam the julienned vegetables and the green beans in separate saucepans of salted water, making sure they stay crisp.*

Crisp Vegetables

5. Chop the shallot and spread it in the bottom of a greased baking dish. Pour in the fish stock and the vermouth. Strew with the saffron and a little salt and pepper. Fill the brill fillets with the julienned vegetables.

6. Place the filled fish fillets in the baking dish and bake in the oven for 30 minutes. Arrange the fish fillets on a serving platter. Add the crème fraîche to the cooking liquid, reduce for a few minutes, then add the lemon juice. Pour the sauce over the fish fillets and serve.

Sole Fillets

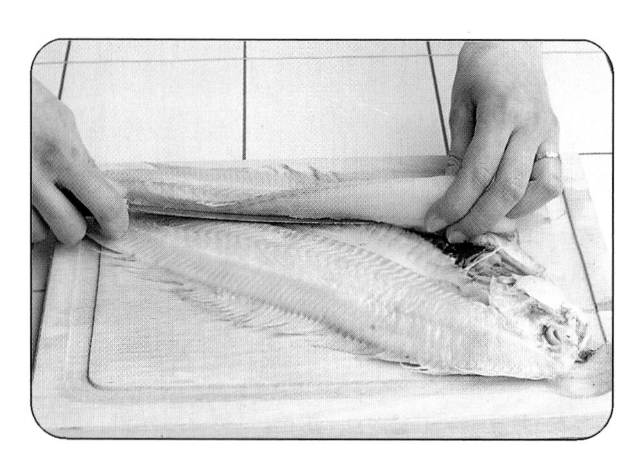

1. Fillet the soles if necessary (see basic recipe), and finely chop the shallots.

Ingredients:
2 soles
2 shallots
¾ cup/200 ml fish stock (see basic recipe)
7 oz/200 g button mushrooms
2 tomatoes
1 clove garlic
1 tbsp olive oil
1 glass dry white wine
4 tbsp crème fraîche
salt and pepper

Serves 4
Preparation time: 20 minutes
Cooking time: 30 minutes
Difficulty: ✯ ✯

2. Grease a baking dish, sprinkle in the shallots, cut up the sole fillets and place them in it.

In French, a *bastidon* is not only a small, fortified house, it is also a kind of enclosed valley, fresh and green, a charming place of repose that greatly contributes to the beauty of hot Provence.
Sole has the habit of burrowing its way into the sand to escape from predators. It is caught with nets in northern waters. In this case, it has been transported by magical culinary arts to Provence. If sole cannot be obtained, use brill, a fish with exquisitely delicate flesh.
To save time and simplify your task, ask your fish retailer to fillet the fish.
The bed of shallots is voluptuously aromatic and will flavor the whole dish. Accompany the soles with green vegetables, steamed potatoes or rice. Easy to prepare, Sole Fillets Bastidon is a light dish will lend elegance to both festive occasions and family meals.
Our wine expert is of the opinion that the refined succulence of sole calls for a very gentle wine; he suggests a Savennières.

3. Pour the fish stock into the pan. Clean, slice and add the mushrooms, and lightly salt them.

4. Seed and crush the tomatoes; peel and chop the garlic. Combine the garlic, tomatoes and olive oil, then spoon this mixture over the fillets and pour in the glass of white wine.

Bastidon

5. Bake in a medium oven for 20 minutes. Arrange the sole fillets on a plate, keeping them hot.

6. In a saucepan, reduce the liquid in which the fish was cooked by half. Stir in the crème fraîche and let the sauce thicken. When ready, pour the sauce over the fish and reheat briefly in the oven. Arrange the fillets on a serving platter interspersed with mounds of crushed tomato and sliced mushrooms. Serve hot.

Crown of

1. *Shell the shrimp. Sauté the heads and shells in a saucepan that has been brushed with olive oil. Add the chopped shallots.*

Ingredients:
32 gamba shrimp
olive oil
1 oz/30 g shallots
½ glass white wine
⅔ cup/150 ml
crème fraîche
3½ tbsp/50 g butter
2 lb 3 oz/1 kg
tomatoes
salt and pepper

Serves 4
Preparation time: 30 minutes
Cooking time: 35 minutes
Difficulty: ★

2. *Pour in the white wine. Add salt, pepper and a glass of water.*

Gambas are large gray shrimp, 7 to 9 inches (15-20 cm) long, which are caught in the depths of the Mediterranean and Atlantic. Much favored in Spanish and Asian cookery, gambas have a pronounced flavor. If they are not available, other large shrimp can be used without the recipe losing any of its exotic appeal.
Our chef offers a few words of advice to help make this dish a success: The pan in which the shrimp are are fried should scarcely contain any oil. Just dip a brush in oil to grease it. If you have the chance, perhaps at a picnic in the open, grill the gambas on a barbecue. The crushed tomatoes should only be warmed slightly in the olive oil, rather than cooked. They can also be seasoned with chopped basil.
For a superior and succulent sauce, squeeze the heads of the gambas to extract the coral from them and add it to the sauce, one of our chef's little secrets. Do not forget to blend the sauce briefly just before serving. You will find that the sauce becomes remarkably smooth and truly marvelous.
Our wine expert suggests a Chablis, noting that the slightly green reflections in your wine glass splendidly complement the red of the gambas.

3. *Now stir in the crème fraîche and reduce the sauce by half. Strain it through a sieve, then vigorously whisk in the butter. Set the sauce aside.*

4. *Skin and seed the tomatoes, and cut them into small even pieces.*

Grilled Gambas

5. Fry the tails of the shrimp in a frying pan with a little olive oil. Season with salt and pepper.

6. Warm the crushed tomatoes in some olive oil and season with salt and pepper. Mound them in the center of a plate and arrange the gamba tails in a crown shape on top. Pour the sauce around the edge of the plate and serve hot.

Crayfish in

1. Peel the pearl onions and stud 1 with the cloves. Flute and slice the carrot, and chop the celery. Put together the bouquet garni.

Ingredients:
4 lb 6 oz/2 kg crayfish
pearl onions
2 cloves
3 carrots
1 celery stalk
1 bouquet garni: thyme, bay leaf, dill
½ bottle white wine
juice of 1 lemon
1 tsp coarsely-ground pepper
2 shallots
2 tbsp/30 ml white vinegar
6½ tbsp/100 ml crème fraîche
10 tbsp/150 g butter
salt and pepper

Serves 6
Preparation time: 20 minutes
Cooking time: 20 minutes
Difficulty: ★

2. Bring a saucepan of water to a boil. Add half the white wine, the lemon juice, vegetables and bouquet garni. Season with salt and the coarsely ground pepper.

Crayfish have been highly regarded for a long time. It would seem that they were eaten by people in rural areas as early as the Middle Ages. They are becoming increasingly rare today, which is a great shame, as these freshwater crustaceans are delicious. The very best crayfish are those with red claws that are found in Auvergne. They are particularly refined in taste and therefore much sought-after.

Crayfish can be cooked in many ways—as a gratin or a pie, with cream, in a croustade, or marinated. Their intestines must be removed if the flesh is to maintain its delicate flavor. Gut the crayfish with great care so that the intestine does not break open.

Our chef has given a personal touch to this recipe by adding dill, celery and other herbs with subtle aromas. Mixed together they create a harmonious flavor.

The butter, well-chilled, should be added to the sauce in small pieces. Just before serving, blend the beurre blanc to give the sauce volume and a slightly frothy texture.

If crayfish can not be obtained, replace them with langoustines; they make a very pleasant alternative. Crayfish in Beurre Blanc will give much delight to fine gourmets. To crown this culinary triumph, follow the advice of our wine expert and serve a Meursault Les Gouttes d'Or.

3. Let the broth boil for 10 minutes, then place the crayfish in it. Cook for another 10 minutes.

4. Finely chop the shallots. Place them in a saucepan. Add the rest of the white wine and the vinegar, and reduce to ¼ its original volume.

Beurre Blanc

5. Stir in the crème fraîche. Let the sauce thicken, then whisk in the butter and adjust the seasoning.

6. Drain the crayfish and shell the tails. Arrange them on a serving platter. Serve with the vegetables and beurre blanc.

John Dory in

1. Carefully fillet the John Dory and remove its skin (see basic recipe).

Ingredients:

1 John Dory weighing 3 lb 5 oz/1.5 kg
3 shallots
Champagne Veuve Cliquot Carte Jaune
10½ oz/300 g chanterelle mushrooms
10½ oz/300 g oyster mushrooms
6½ tbsp/100 g butter
⅔ cup/150 ml heavy cream
salt and pepper

Serves 4
Preparation time: 15 minutes
Cooking time: 20 minutes
Difficulty: ★

The John Dory is easily recognized by the large round spot on both its sides. Legend has it that these are the thumbprints of St.Peter, who drew the fish out of the water on Christ's instructions in order to take a coin from its mouth to pay him a tribute at Capernaum.

This is one of the best saltwater fish. Its flesh is white and firm, rich in protein, phosphorus and potassium, and its taste is subtle and aromatic. The John Dory is a medium-fat fish.

Take care if you are filleting it yourself: A wound inflicted by the bones quickly becomes infected, as this otherwise perfect fish takes its revenge! Turbot or salmon would also be good choices to prepare in this manner.

Chanterelles need longer to cook than oyster mushrooms, so start cooking them two or three minutes earlier. You can also use other mushrooms for this recipe. Choose wild ones or cultivated varieties, as you wish.

John Dory in Champagne Sauce is a real "open sesame" for the gates of a gastronomic paradise. The delicate nature of this fish calls for an extremely gentle wine: a Champagne Veuve Cliquot Carte Jaune.

2. Peel and finely chop 2 of the shallots. Generously butter a baking dish, sprinkle in the shallots and place the John Dory fillets in it.

3. Pour in the champagne, add a little salt and pepper and bake in a medium oven for 15 minutes.

4. Thoroughly clean all the mushrooms, and finely chop the remaining shallot.

Champagne Sauce

5. Sauté the mushrooms, starting with the chanterelles, in a frying pan with 3 tbsp/50 g of the butter. Add salt, pepper and the shallot.

6. Reduce the cooking liquid from the John Dory fillets by half, then pour in the cream. Stir, adjust the seasoning if necessary, again reduce by half and whisk the rest of the butter into the sauce. Strain it through a fine sieve, pour over the fish fillets and serve very hot with the sautéed mushrooms.

Sea Bass and

1. *Scale and fillet the sea bass (see basic recipe). Use a knife to cut the fillet in half. Keep the skin on a little of the flesh, and cut the rest into thin slices. Chill them. Blanch the spinach leaves, keeping them very crisp.*

Ingredients:
1 sea bass weighing 1 lb 12 oz/800 g
5¼ oz/150 g salmon fillet
3½ oz/100 g spinach
2 egg whites
1 egg yolk
2 cups/500 ml crème fraîche
1 shallot
1 carrot
1 bunch of chives
1 truffle
1 tbsp Meaux mustard
4½ tbsp/70 g butter
salt and pepper

Serves 4
Preparation time: 35 minutes
Cooking time: 20 minutes
Difficulty: ★ ★

2. *Purée the skinless pieces of sea bass. Add the egg whites, egg yolk and a little salt and pepper, and mix thoroughly. Then add ¾ cup/200 ml of the crème fraîche, blend again and refrigerate the purée.*

Ballotine is the lovely name given to rolls of boneless meat or fish, in this case bass and salmon, which are filled with vegetables and rolled up before being cooked. Preparing them requires some dexterity and patience, but these Sea Bass and Salmon Ballotines will enhance your meals with their glamour and aroma.
To save time, ask the fish retailer to fillet the sea bass, leaving the skin on.
The fish purée should be smooth and satiny. For it to succeed completely, the meat of the fish should be quite cold before it is puréed in a food processor. Consider preparing the purée the night before to make your job easier. It keeps very well in the refrigerator.
Tie tight knots to seal the ballotines hermetically. The plastic wrap must not come undone during the cooking process if the dish is to succeed.
The truffle adds its sumptuous darkness to the beauty of this dish, though *trompette de la morte* mushrooms could also be used to add a touch of black.
Now everything is ready to serve. This dish mixes the crisp with the smooth. It is ideal for an intimate *tete à tete*, and is a good way to shake off the winter blues, being rich in calories, phosphorus and iodine.
Our wine expert recommends a Pouilly-Fumé. The velvety finish of this fine wine from the Loire will be a marvelous accompaniment for this seafood dish.

3. *Peel and finely chop the shallot and sauté in a saucepan with 1 tbsp butter. Peel and chop the carrot and chives, and add both to the shallot. Simmer with the lid on. Once cooked, let this mixture cool, then stir it into the sea bass purée.*

4. *Lay down a piece of plastic wrap on a work surface and place on it a slice of salmon, a slice of truffle and a slice of sea bass with the skin on. Using a pastry bag, squeeze the purée along 4½ in/11 cm of the fish slices, then roll everything up snugly in the plastic wrap.*

Salmon Ballotines

5. Tie the ends of the rolls firmly. Place a double boiler over heat and steam the ballotines for about 10 minutes.

6. Bring the rest of the crème fraîche to a boil, add salt, pepper and the Meaux mustard, stir vigorously and reduce the mixture for several minutes. When the sauce is smooth, whisk in the remaining butter. Unwrap the ballotines and serve with the mustard sauce.

Coquilles St.-Jacques

1. *Chop the onions finely. Remove the rind from the bacon and cut the bacon into small pieces. Sauté the onions in a saucepan with the lard. When they start to become transparent, add the chopped bacon and cook over gentle heat.*

Ingredients:
12 scallops
2 medium-sized onions
7 oz/200 g bacon
2 tbsp lard
1 glass white wine
2 potatoes
3 tbsp seaweed
1 leek
salt and pepper

Serves 4
Preparation time: 25 minutes
Cooking time: 15 minutes
Difficulty: ★

2. *Add the glass of wine and 2 glasses of water, and cook for a few minutes.*

Coquilles Saint-Jacques is the elegant French term for scallops. This method of preparation may require quite a novel shopping trip for seaweed, which one could call the vegetable of the sea. Of the countless varieties, samphire, saltwort and chondrus crispus are generally not difficult to obtain. The idea of preparing the scallops surrounded by their natural environment is both original and delicious. What is more, this salad from the sea is rich in protein, vitamins, minerals and iodine, which is indispensable for the correct function of the thyroid. The taste of the seaweed combines wonderfully with the subtle flavor of the scallops.
This lovely winter entrée is easy to make. Take your time cutting everything into small pieces; the results will be worth it. Pay careful attention to cooking times. They are all very brief, especially for the scallops, which should just be brought to a boil, then removed from the heat. It is important that they remain firm if they are to keep their exquisite flavor.
Coquilles Saint-Jacques à la Serge might be an option for New Years' parties, a time for effusive feelings, family reunions, shared joys and long pleasurable meals. These scallops will bring a regional French delight to your table.
Our wine expert suggests a Meursault La Les Gouttes d'Or

3. *Peel and finely dice the potatoes. Add them to the bacon mixture and season with pepper, but taste before adding salt, as the bacon will also release salt.*

4. *While this broth is cooking, carefully clean the seaweed, drain and finely shred. Chop the leek greens.*

à la Serge

5. When the potatoes are about ¾ cooked, add the chopped leek and the seaweed, and simmer for a few more minutes.

6. Pour this boiling mixture onto the scallops, bring briefly to a boil, remove from the heat and serve.

Five Fish

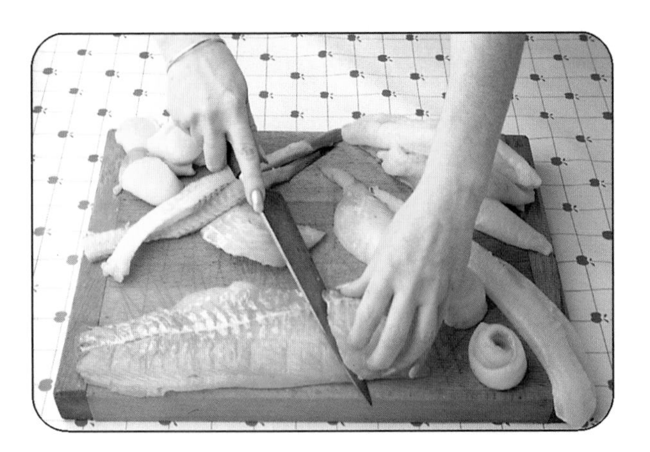

1. Fillet all the fish. Cut 4 large slices of haddock.

Ingredients:
10½ oz/300 g haddock
10½ oz/300 g monkfish
8¾ oz/250 g sole fillets
4 lb 6 oz/2 kg white-heart cabbage
1 head of garlic
3 or 4 star anise
1 cup/250 ml milk
8 mussels
4 scallops
¾ cup/200 ml fish stock (see basic recipe) or 1 fish stock cube
¾ cup/200 ml crème fraîche
6½ tbsp/100 g butter
salt and pepper

Serves 4
Preparation time: 40 minutes
Cooking time: 25 minutes
Difficulty: ★

2. Blanch the cabbage, changing the water twice. Finish cooking it in lightly salted water, making sure it stays slightly crisp.

Sometimes we are so seduced by sophisticated dishes that we forget the basic, familiar pleasures of the table. The cabbage, popular in "country cooking," has not always found its way into more elegant dining rooms. This distinctive recipe gives us the chance to rediscover the virtues of this delicious vegetable.

Our chef's recipe is one for all seasons, as cabbage is available all year round. Cabbage takes quite a long time to cook, but it can be done in advance. Once cooked, it keeps well in the refrigerator.

The star anise will not only lend flavor to this dish, but also balance the garlic, with which it is subtly combined.

The ideal for this recipe is to mix four or five different fish, preferably including one smoked fish in your selection; otherwise, you have a free hand. Keep in mind that each fish needs a different length of time to cook. Longer-cooking monkfish should be sliced thinly; cod cooks quickly, so cut it into thick slices. Also slice the haddock before cooking it.

Five Fish Embeurrée will enrapture any fish-lover, and you will be pleased to have been able to provide them with such a culinary pleasure.

Our wine expert suggests a Sancerre Blanc: The splendid aromas of the Sauvignon grape will combine with the nobility of this dish to make it truly festive.

3. Peel the cloves of garlic. Blanch them, changing the water twice, then add the star anise.

4. Poach the haddock in the milk with a little pepper.

Embeurrée

5. Place the sole and monkfish fillets, the mussels and the scallops in a pan, pour in the fish stock and poach.

6. Remove the cloves of garlic from the water, place them in a saucepan with the crème fraîche, blend thoroughly and add the butter. Arrange the cabbage on a deep serving platter, place the assortment of fish and crustaceans on it, pour over the garlic cream sauce and serve very hot.

Weakfish

1. *Peel and coarsely chop the onions. Sauté them in a saucepan with the butter.*

Ingredients:
1 weakfish weighing 2 lb 10 oz/1.2 kg
2 onions
6½ tbsp/100 g butter
1 tsp tomato paste
6½ tbsp/100 ml wine vinegar
2 cups/500 ml red wine
1⅔ cups/400 ml Pineau
1 bunch white grapes
salt and pepper

Serves 4
Preparation time: 30 minutes
Cooking time: 30 minutes
Difficulty: ★ ★

2. *When the onions are browned, add the tomato paste and stir vigorously.*

Pineau is an apéritif made only in Charente. It is a true nectar, especially if you give credence to the legend that it was created by chance, or, if you prefer, by the will of the gods. Last century, a wine-grower of Charentes, finding that he was short of barrels during a very good harvest, put some of the grape juice into an old cask still containing Cognac. By the time he realized this, it was too late to do anything about it, so he left the mixture to mature. This is how Pineau was created; and its fame spread rapidly throughout the whole region.

Weakfish, also known as sea trout, is caught off the island of Olèron and at the mouth of the Gironde river in France, and along the eastern coast of North America. You could also use sea bass, turbot, tautog or cunner in this recipe.

If you are worried that the cooked fish could disintegrate when handled, lay them on some greased aluminum foil, then in a couscous kettle or steamer.

For those not from this Atlantic region, here is the chance to explore some of the products from Charente and to continue this magnificent gastronomic tour of France. Your guests will be very appreciative of the elegance and lightness of this dish, and a meal of fish is always welcome.

Our wine expert suggests a Graves Blanc, a wine too little regarded: Its aroma suggests the salt of the ocean.

3. *Pour in the wine vinegar, reduce for 5 minutes, and then add the red wine. Bring to a boil again for about 15 minutes.*

4. *Add the Pineau, season with salt and pepper, and simmer for about 15 minutes. When ready, strain the sauce through a sieve, simmer for a few moments, add a knob of butter and set the sauce aside.*

with Pineau

5. Fillet the weakfish (see basic recipe) and cut 4 large slices.

6. Place the fish in a steamer, add a little salt and pepper and steam for about 15 minutes. Meanwhile, add the grapes to the sauce and heat gently. Arrange the fish on a serving platter, cover with the sauce and grapes, and serve hot.

Mouclade

Ingredients:
4 lb 6 oz/2 kg
mussels
4 shallots
6 sprigs of parsley
1 tbsp butter
3 glasses of dry
white wine
1 glass Pineau
2 egg yolks
1 cup/250 ml
heavy cream
1 pinch of saffron
salt and pepper

1. Peel the shallots and finely chop them along with the parsley. Sauté the shallots in a saucepan with the butter. Once they are slightly browned, add the thoroughly cleaned mussels.

Serves 8
Preparation time: 20 minutes
Cooking time: 25 minutes
Difficulty: ★

2. Now add the chopped parsley and season lightly with salt and pepper.

Mouclade is one of the gastronomic gems of the Aunis and Saintonge regions of France. Perhaps you have had the chance to taste and enjoy this delicious mussel dish, one of the numerous treasures of this region, during your travels. Now you can enjoy making it for your family and friends.

If you like colorful flavors and aromas, it will interest you to know that this dish traditionally used curry. Here, our chef has chosen to replace the curry with saffron, which lends the sauce both a sumptuous yellow color and a delicious flavor.

The time needed to prepare this recipe depends on your skill in washing (or sometimes scraping) and shelling the mussels. There are no great difficulties involved, however, be careful when reducing the mussel stock. This will form the basis of the sauce, so it is important not to spoil it.

A nice touch is to heat the serving platter so that the mussels stay warm until the moment you serve them to your guests.

Delicious, easy and quick to make, Mouclade will give you the chance to offer your guests a festival of subtle flavors and aromas. What is more, it is also very nourishing, owing to the high iodine and protein content of the mussels.

Our wine expert feels that a coastal wine will enhance the iodine aroma of the Mouclade. He recommends a Muscadet sur lie.

3. Pour in the white wine and Pineau, cover the pan, and steam until the mussels open. Stir occasionally.

4. Once the mussels have opened, strain the cooking liquid through a sieve and reduce by half. While doing this, shell the mussels and place them on the serving platter resting in their shell.

5. Combine the egg yolks and the heavy cream and stir briskly.

6. Add the cream and egg yolk mixture to the piping hot stock along with the saffron. Whisk vigorously and remove from heat. Pour the sauce over the mussels and serve very hot.

Tuna Tournedos

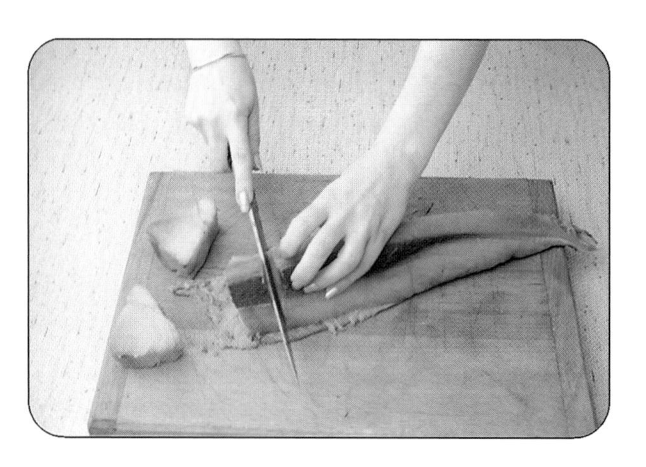

1. *Cut 4 pieces of tuna fillet the size of tournedos (see glossary). Soak the bone marrow in cold water to purge it.*

Ingredients:
1 tuna fillet, about 2 lb 3 oz/1 kg
3½ oz/100 g bone marrow
3 shallots
1 tbsp tomato paste
2 cups/500 ml red wine
10½ oz/300 ml Banyuls
½ cup/120 g butter
2 potatoes
salt and pepper

Serves 4
Preparation time: 25 minutes
Cooking time: 30 minutes
Difficulty: ★

2. *Peel and finely chop the shallots, then sauté them with 1 tbsp butter. When they are slightly browned, add the tomato paste. Stir vigorously.*

Used in cooking since ancient times, tuna is often neglected on restaurant menus. It is worthy of being served at the best tables, and deserves to be more highly regarded. The ancient Greeks already knew about the long voyages made by this migratory fish, which tends to travel in a compact shoal. In Provence at the turn of the last century, watchmen on the coast used to announce its approach with blasts on a trumpet. A fatty fish, tuna possesses a high energy value and is rich in protein, phosphorus, iodine, iron and the vitamins A and B.

Everything about this seafood dish makes one think of red meat: the color and texture of tuna, the bone marrow that traditionally accompanies rib steak, and even the Banyuls (a fortified red wine) used in the sauce. Our chef suggests Atlantic bluefin tuna, caught in the Mediterranean and in the Bay of Biscay, to stay in keeping with the theme of tournedos. There are of course other varieties of tuna that are easy to obtain, and the albacore is found most frequently.

Serve Tuna Tournedos with Marrow very hot, accompanied by sliced potatoes, and consume immediately, as this dish does benefit from waiting.

Our wine expert feels that the combination of marrow and tuna is a good opportunity to open a Saint-Nicholas-de-Bourgeuil, a light red wine with a slight raspberry aroma.

3. *Pour in the red wine, stir until the tomato paste is diluted and simmer over gentle heat for about 15 minutes. Season lightly with salt and pepper.*

4. *Add the Banyuls, simmer for another 5 to 10 minutes and adjust the seasoning. Strain through a fine sieve, whisk in 2 tbsp butter, and put the sauce aside.*

with Marrow

5. When the marrow is purged, poach it in lightly salted water.

6. Fry the tuna tournedos in a pan with the rest of the butter. Add salt and pepper and make sure the tuna does not dry out. Arrange the tournedos on a serving platter and place a round of bone marrow on each. Garnish with sliced fried potatoes and accompany with the sauce. Serve very hot.

Gourmet Cunner

1. Fillet the cunners (see basic recipe) and set them aside. Clean and dice all the vegetables: the eggplant, zucchini, sweet red and green peppers and onion.

Ingredients:
2 cunners
1 eggplant
2 zucchini
2 sweet red peppers
2 sweet green peppers
1 onion
6½ tbsp/100 ml oil
1 fish bouillon cube
¾ cup/200 g crème fraîche
6½ tbsp/100 g butter
1 bunch of chives
salt and pepper

Serves 4
Preparation time: 45 minutes
Cooking time: 35 minutes
Difficulty: ★

2. Sauté the chopped onion in a frying pan with the oil. Do not let them become too brown.

The chives grown in kitchen gardens, with their pungent flavor—more refined and discreet then that of onion—have their origins very far away. This aromatic plant, which belongs to the same family as garlic and onions, originally comes from China, and it is still used often in Southeast Asian cookery. Closer to home, chives are used fresh and finely minced to flavor omelets, salads or cheeses.

This dish is easy to prepare, the only trick being to make sure the cunner fillets are not overcooked. This would make the flesh too soft, and it might break up while preparing it for serving, which would be a great shame.

Any fish can be used for this recipe. Serve it hot as soon as it is ready, accompanied by the crispy vegetables. Another advantage of this meal, which is rich in vitamin A and calcium, is that it can be reheated over gentle heat without any problems. Gourmet Cunner in Cream with Chives will bring an element of novelty to your everyday meals.

Our wine expert cautions that the exuberant flavor of chives has the roguish habit of drowning the flavor of a wine. Try a Saint-Véran, a lovely white wine doubtless able to hold its own.

3. Add the sweet peppers. Sauté gently.

4. Add the eggplant and zucchini and season with salt and pepper. Sauté over low heat, covered, for 15 minutes, stirring occasionally.

in Cream with Chives

5. Place the cunner fillets in a lightly buttered baking dish and sprinkle with salt and pepper. Dissolve the bouillon cube in 1¼ cups/300 ml water and pour it in. Cook in a hot oven.

6. Strain the cooking liquid into a saucepan and reduce it by half. Stir in the crème fraîche and let it thicken, then whisk in the butter. Arrange the fillets on a serving platter, coat with sauce and accompany with mounds of ratatouille. Sprinkle the fillets with chopped chives.

Oysters and Sea Bass à la

1. Open the oysters and poach them in the fish bouillon dissolved in ¾ cup/200 ml of water and the vermouth. Retain the cooking liquid.

Ingredients:
16 oysters
2 sea bass fillets
1 fish bouillon cube
2 glasses Noilly vermouth
4 lb 6 oz/2 kg spinach
¾ cup/200 ml crème fraîche
3½ tbsp/50 g butter
1 tbsp salmon caviar
salt and pepper

Serves 4
Preparation time: 35 minutes
Cooking time: 25 minutes
Difficulty: ★ ★

2. Clean the spinach thoroughly, remove the stems and cook it briefly in salted water. Drain and chill.

The Atlantic sea bass is also called sea perch because of its resemblance to perch. This exquisite fish is in fact a voracious predator. It is relatively rare, which accounts for its high price. As they are so similar, the bass can be replaced by perch.
Use fresh, small oysters that are tightly closed; if they are open, they are not fresh. Also, remember that they do not benefit from prolonged cooking: more than a few seconds will make them become rubbery.
To flatten the slices of sea bass without damaging them, lay the fish between two pieces of plastic wrap. Straining the cooking liquid through a fine sieve to eliminate any impurities, and blending the sauce just before it is served, will improve its quality.
Spinach, which has a cleansing effect on the intestines, is also good for anemia, containing iron and vitamin B. This hot dish is also excellent served with avocado purée. However, this can not be reheated.
As a final touch, the salmon caviar will add their sumptuous pink and an elegant refinement of flavor to your meal.
Such a fine dish calls for a fine wine. Our wine expert suggests a Corton-Charlemagne.

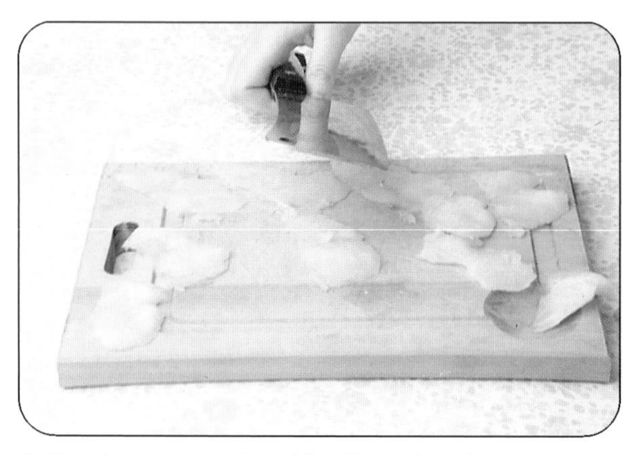

3. Cut the sea bass into thin slices, then flatten them slightly between 2 sheets of plastic wrap as described.

4. Grease an ovenproof dish well. Wrap the oysters in the slices of sea bass fillet and place them in the dish. Season with salt and pepper.

Florentine with Vermouth

5. Pour the liquid retained from cooking the oysters over the fish rolls. Cook in a hot oven for about 10 minutes. Remove the rolls and reduce the remaining liquid to ¼ of its initial volume.

6. Whisk in the crème fraîche. Let the sauce thicken for some minutes, then whisk in the butter. Cover a serving platter with the sauce. Arrange the rolls on a bed of spinach, garnish with salmon caviar and serve very hot.

Spiny Lobster in

1. *Cut the lobsters in half lengthwise. Using a fork, remove as much of the coral from the head as possible. Remove the intestine and stomach.*

Ingredients:
2 spiny lobsters
2 shallots
chervil
parsley
2 cloves of garlic
1 glass dry white wine
1 small glass Noilly vermouth
2 tomatoes
juice of 4 mandarin oranges
6½ tbsp/100 ml Mandarine liqueur
1 tbsp paprika
saffron
5 tbsp/70 g butter
salt and pepper

Serves 4
Preparation time: 30 minutes
Cooking time: 20 minutes
Difficulty: ★

2. *Chop the shallots, parsley, chervil and garlic. Salt and pepper the pieces of lobster and sear them in a frying pan with oil. Add the chopped herbs and shallots.*

Before becoming a dish for ceremonial occasions, the spiny lobster already had a good reputation. This crustacean, which lives on rocky seabeds, has become increasingly rare today, which of course, has raised their price and their desirability. It is caught in the English Channel, the eastern Atlantic and the western Mediterranean. If you use Maine lobster instead of spiny lobster, the recipe will lose none of its character. Choose lobsters that move their tails vigorously, a sure sign of freshness.

After cutting open the lobster, it is important to remove the stomach, situated in the head, as well as the intestine. If the lobster is cooked for too long, it will lose its tenderness. Cook rapidly at the start to keep the flesh firm.

The intoxicating aroma of the Mandarine liqueur should remain light and subtle, so be sure to use only a moderate amount. Our chef suggests using pepper or pink peppercorns in place of paprika, as a variation. Once you have added the butter, the sauce must not boil any more. Serve hot as soon as it is ready.

Spiny Lobster in Mandarin Orange Sauce is a superbly colored dish. The balanced combination of sweet, salty and sour produces a sparkling array of flavors, and deserves a place of honor at your most important dinner parties.

To further enhance the harmonious color scheme, our wine expert suggests you open a good bottle of Veuve Cliquot Rosé Champagne, to the delight of all.

3. *Mix in the white wine, vermouth, finely chopped tomatoes, mandarin orange juice and ½ of the Mandarine liqueur. Season with salt and pepper.*

4. *Add the paprika and saffron. Turn over the lobster and cook for 5 minutes.*

Mandarin Orange Sauce

5. Remove the lobster from the liquid and keep them hot on a plate. Empty the sauce into a saucepan and blend with a hand mixer. Add the butter and coral and blend once more. Adjust the seasoning if necessary.

6. Stir in the rest of the Mandarine liqueur and pour the sauce over the lobster pieces. Serve very hot.

Sole Spirals with

1. *Separate the eggs and blend the chilled salmon in a food processor with the egg whites. Season with salt and pepper, then add the cream, tomato paste, and cherry brandy. Blend until it forms a firm mousse.*

Ingredients:
1 large sole
5¼ oz/150 g salmon fillet
2 eggs
⅔ cup/150 ml heavy cream
1 tbsp tomato paste
3½ tbsp/50 ml cherry brandy
1 tbsp green peppercorns
salt and pepper
For the sauce:
3½ tbsp/50 ml white wine
3½ tbsp/50 ml white vinegar
1 shallot
juice of 1 lemon
½ cup/120 ml heavy cream
chives; chervil
1 tbsp blanched spinach
salt and pepper

Serves 4
Preparation time: 35 minutes
Cooking time: 30 minutes
Difficulty: ⋆ ⋆

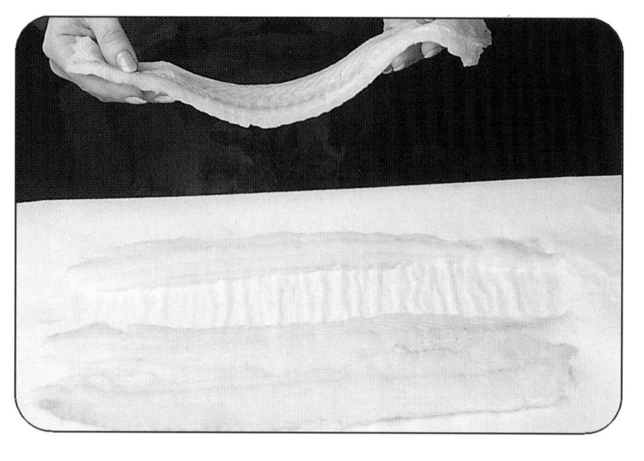

2. *Remove the skin from the sole. Cut into 4 fillets (see basic recipe), beat them lightly and place them side by side on a sheet of parchment paper sprinkled with water. Season with salt and pepper.*

The sole, a fish with a venerable past, has very delicate flesh and is a recommended food for infants because it is lean and has a rich mineral content. This particular recipe is a little tricky to make, but very rewarding; just follow our chef's instructions carefully to ensure success. After filleting the sole, remove the nerves and beat the fillets to break up any nerve strands to prevent the fish from shrinking during cooking.
The salmon fillet should be placed in the freezer. This is essential for the texture of the mousse. Salmon can whiten when it is cooked, so intensify the color of the mousse by adding tomato paste.
Coarsely chop the spinach so that it purées more easily. If the green peppercorns have been in brine, make sure to rinse them in water before using them. Mix the egg yolks with a little cold water before adding them to the sauce, off the heat.
This dish cannot be reheated. Too prolonged cooking ruins the sole's flavor and causes it to lose its delicacy and tenderness. It can, however, be served cold the next day along with an herb mayonnaise.
Rich and tasty, this entrée is ideal for social gatherings or important dinners
To bring out the unique flavors of both the sole and the peppercorns, our wine expert recommends a fine wine from Alsace, a Gewürztraminer.

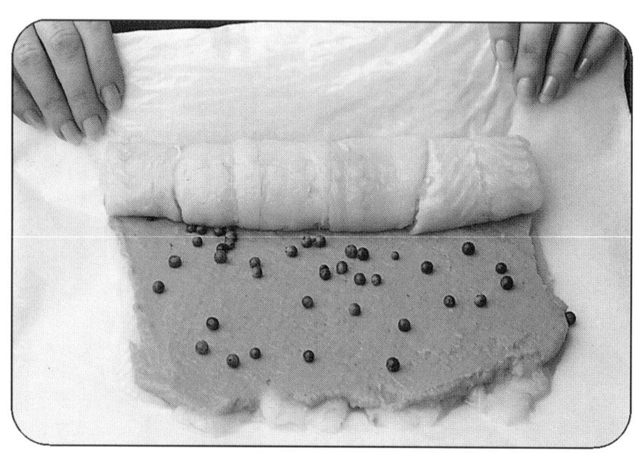

3. *Using a palette knife, spread the salmon mousse over the sole fillets. Sprinkle on the green peppercorns and roll up the fillets lengthwise.*

4. *Tie up the fish roll in the parchment paper and steam it for about 20 minutes.*

Green Peppercorns

5. For the sauce, chop the shallots, chives, chervil and spinach. Blanch the spinach briefly. Pour the white wine and vinegar into a saucepan and add the chopped shallots. Reduce by ¾, then add the cream, lemon juice, and salt and pepper.

6. Add the chives, chervil and blanched spinach to the sauce and blend. Bring to a boil. Add the egg yolks and mix once more. Adjust the seasoning and set the sauce aside. Unwrap the fish roll and slice it. Pour the sauce on a serving platter. Arrange the sole spirals on the sauce, and serve very hot.

Skate with Curry

1. Peel the carrots and clean the leeks thoroughly, then cut into julienne.

Ingredients:
1 skate wing,
1 lb 11 oz-2 lb/
800-900 g
10½ oz/300 g carrots
10½ oz/300 g leeks
1 tbsp curry powder
1¼ cups/300 ml oil
6½ tbsp/100 ml
fish stock (see
basic recipe) or
1 fish stock cube
13 tbsp/200 g butter
6½ tbsp/100 ml
olive oil
1 bunch of chives
salt and pepper

Serves 4
Preparation time: 25 minutes
Cooking time: 35 minutes
Difficulty: ★ ★

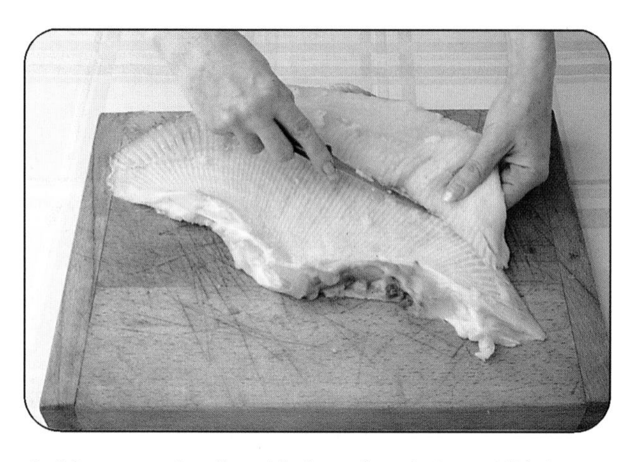

2. After removing the skin from the skate, cut it into fillets (see basic recipe).

Fried vegetables flavored with curry give this dish an Indian touch that transform it. The skate, bathed in these exotic aromas, will appear in a completely different light. It is delightful to become reacquainted with it, and to discover it afresh at the same time. The winter can be depressing; let yourself be transported to sunny climes by the aromas released in your kitchen while preparing this fabulous feast.
When the julienned vegetables start to brown, it is time to remove them from the oil in which they are cooking. Use some absorbent paper to drain the vegetables and the skate. This will make everything lighter, a great quality in the field of cookery.
Monkfish is also suitable for this recipe. But, as the skate is currently experiencing a renaissance of sorts, and because its flavor is well worth it, our chef gives it first preference. Skate with Curry and Fried Vegetables is an original fish recipe that is economical, and will give family meals a festive air while doing friends honor.
Our wine expert suggests a combination that is certainly surprising, but also unforgettable: Drink a Gewürztraminer with this dish.

3. Salt and pepper the skate fillets, sprinkle them with curry powder and place in the refrigerator. Fry the julienned carrot in a saucepan with oil and drain on a piece of absorbent paper.

4. Now fry the julienned leeks. Drain them on absorbent paper as well.

and Fried Vegetables

5. In a saucepan, add the rest of the curry powder to the fish stock. Reduce by ¾, then whisk in the butter. Put the sauce aside.

6. Just before it is time to serve, fry the skate fillets in a frying pan with the olive oil. Pour the curry sauce on a serving platter, arrange the skate fillets on it, and mound fried vegetables on top of each skate filet. Garnish with sprigs of chives.

Cod

1. *Cut the zucchini into thin slices, and sauté them in a frying pan with a little olive oil. Put aside.*

Ingredients:
1 lb 4 oz/600 g cod fillets
10½ oz/300 g zucchini
¾ cup/200 ml olive oil
juice of one lemon
1 lb/500 g tomatoes
1 bunch of basil
1 sprig of thyme
salt and pepper

Serves 4
Preparation time: 25 minutes
Cooking time: 25 minutes
Difficulty: ★ ★

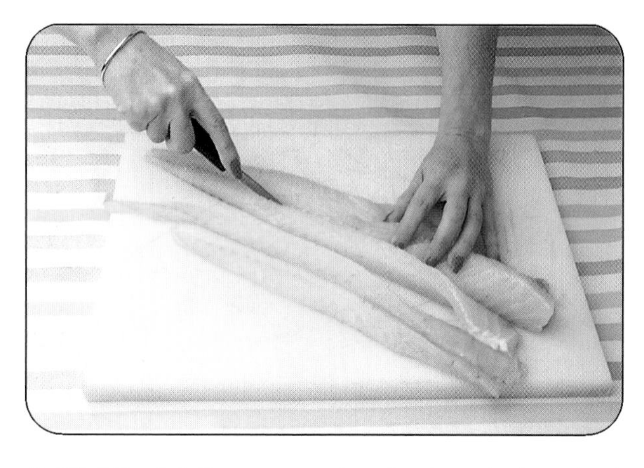

2. *Fillet the fish if necessary (see basic recipe), and cut the fillets into long strips.*

With this recipe our chef presents an imaginative variation on a well-known trio of ingredients: olive oil, lemon and tomato. It is always a winner, delicious and good to eat. The tartness of the lemon brings out the best in the fish, elegantly enhancing its flavor.
Steaming is a very fast method of cooking and keeps the flavor of the cod concentrated. You can also buy sole or whiting fillets and prepare the fish a day in advance. Keep it in the refrigerator and cook it just before serving. Tomatoes are rich in the vitamins A, B and C, and have a strong revitalizing and refreshing effect. What a pleasure to be able to benefit from it!
The cooking times in this recipe are extremely short, making it possible to sit at the table with guests without having to spend long tending the stove.
Cod Spiral is a recipe full of subtlety. Each aroma, each color will open up pleasures that are only enhanced by eating it.
Accompany this meal with a Château-Carbonnieux because, as our wine expert explains, this Graves wine possesses considerable finesse.

3. *Spread out a piece of oven-proof plastic wrap, place a mold on it and arrange the strips of cod around the inside of the mold to create a spiral that entirely fills it.*

4. *Sprinkle with salt and pepper, pour over a little olive oil and the lemon juice, and steam. Skin, seed and crush the tomatoes into a saucepan. Add a little salt and pepper and some basil leaves, and cook this concassé over low heat.*

Spiral

5. When the cod spiral is cooked, arrange it on a serving platter and cover it with zucchini rounds.

6. Add the rest of the olive oil to the crushed tomatoes and adjust the seasoning with a little salt, pepper and chopped basil and thyme to taste. Serve the spiral accompanied by the tomato concassé.

Sea Bass

1. *Bring a saucepan of water to a boil. Scald the sea bass so that the skin can be removed. Gut and trim the fish (see basic recipe).*

Ingredients:
1 sea bass weighing
3 lb 4 oz/1.5 kg
2 fennel bulbs
1 head of lettuce
3½ tbsp/50 ml pastis
1 glass white wine
1 tbsp crème fraîche
béarnaise sauce
(see basic recipe)
salt and pepper

Serves 4
Preparation time: 35 minutes
Cooking time: 30 minutes
Difficulty: ★

2. *Chop the fennel and sauté it in a frying pan with a little olive oil. Lightly salt and pepper.*

MaîtreGaspard was a fisherman from Marseille who opened a fine restaurant in the region. The sea bass recipe that he created is described here just as he prepared it. You will see that it has survived the passage of time for good reason: Its refined flavor is without comparison.

However, some variation is allowed; our chef suggests replacing the strips of fennel with a purée of celery or fennel, for example. When cooking the fennel, take care that it does not brown; it will be all the more delicious if it is crisp.

As accompaniment, serve bulbs of fennel. Slice up the first layers and cook the heart in Greek style (water, white wine, olive oil and saffron). This way it is a veritable feast.

This dish must be served hot and cannot be kept. However, it is much too enticing to have to worry about having leftovers.

The sea bass is a fine fish that deserves to receive the honors due to it. Boil the fish for a few minutes so that the skin can be removed more easily. With Maître Gaspard and his sunny cuisine, it will be in its element and will lend your table a savory distinction.

Our wine expert suggests a white wine from the Bellet hills above the Bay of Angels, a Château de Crémat, for example.

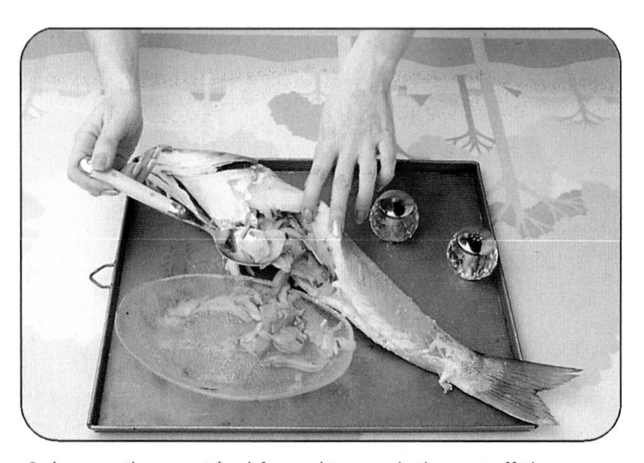

3. *Leave the sautéed fennel to cool, then stuff the sea bass with it.*

4. *Blanch the lettuce leaves slightly. Wrap the sea bass in several leaves.*

"Maître Gaspard"

5. Pour the pastis and white wine over the bass, salt and pepper, then blend in the crème fraîche. Cover with aluminum foil and bake for 20 minutes in a hot oven.

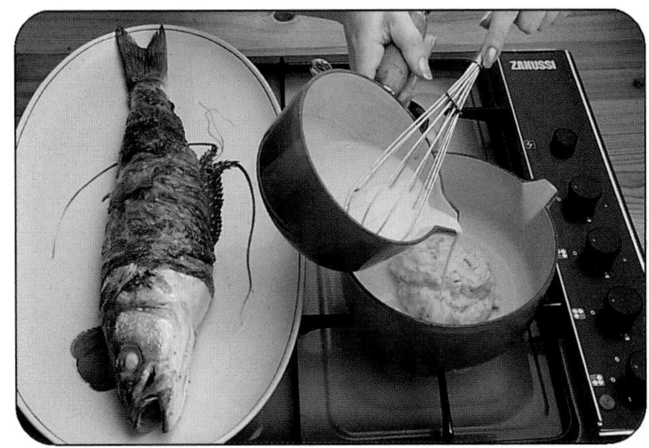

6. Place the sea bass on a serving platter and pour the cooking liquid into a saucepan. Reduce this by half, then pour it into the béarnaise sauce while whisking vigorously. Serve the bass accompanied by this sauce.

Cod Flakes

1. Fillet the fish (see basic recipe) and cut into slices. Chop up the sweet peppers, shallots, fennel and celery. Mince the garlic, parsley and chives. Seed and coarsely chop the tomatoes.

Ingredients:
1 cod, 2 lb 3 oz/1 kg
7 oz/200 g sweet red peppers
2½ oz/75 g shallots
7 oz/200 g fennel
3½ oz/100 g celery
¾ oz/20 g garlic
1¾ oz/50 g parsley
1 oz/25 g chives
6½ tbsp/100 ml oil
1 lb/500 g tomatoes
2 cups/500 ml white wine
½ tsp saffron
2 cups/500 ml fish stock
For the garnish:
1 ¾ oz/50 g celery root
2 ½ oz/75 g sweet peppers
2 ½ oz/75 g zucchini
butter, chervil, salt, pepper

Serves 4
Preparation time: 35 minutes
Cooking time: 30 minutes
Difficulty: ★

Cod is an excellent, all-purpose fish. Available all year round, it is not only good for your figure, being low in fat, but also good for your health because it is full of minerals. It is fairly inexpensive, and can be bought fresh or frozen.

Our chef advises cooking the sauce over low heat so that it does not reduce too far. After simmering the sauce for about thirty minutes, strain it through a sieve. If you find the consistency too thin, continue to reduce it further until it coats a spoon. Give it time to develop a full-bodied range of flavors.

The cod is a delicate fish that does not like to be handled roughly. Take care when cooking it: The pan should not be crowded and it is best to use two spatulas so that you can turn the pieces over easily and gently. A few minutes are enough to cook the cod ; then pour in cold water to stop the cooking process.

Cod Flakes with Aromatic Herbs is a simple and quick way to transform an everyday meal into an extraordinary one.

A wine with iodine aroma grown on the coast will be the perfect companion to this tasty dish. Our wine expert suggests a Muscadet sur lie.

2. Sauté all the chopped vegetables and minced garlic in a large saucepan with the oil. Add the parsley, chives and tomatoes.

3. Mix in the white wine and saffron, then bring to a boil. Season with salt and pepper. Add the fish stock and simmer over low heat for about 30 minutes.

4. Fry the cod fillets in a frying pan with hot oil without them brown. Dice the celery root, peppers and zucchini for the garnish, and sauté briefly in butter.

with Aromatic Herbs

5. Blend the sauce with a hand mixer.

6. Strain the sauce through a sieve to obtain an aromatic broth. Bring this to a boil and reduce by ¾. Cover the bottom of a serving platter with the broth and arrange the cod slices on it. Place some of the vegetables for the garnish on each slice, and decorate with chervil leaves.

Grilled Lobster in

1. *Use a large knife to cut the lobsters in half.*

Ingredients:
2 live lobsters, each
1 lb 5 oz/600 g
1¼ cups/300 g butter
1 bunch of lemon
thyme
1 bunch of parsley
1 lemon
salt and pepper

Serves 4
Preparation time: 15 minutes
Cooking time: 25 minutes
Difficulty: ★

2. *Remove the stomach, as well as the bowel in the center of the tail.*

The tastiest and most sought-after of all crustaceans, lobster is usually reserved for important dinners or special occasions. Our chef's manner of preparation, delicately aromatic, will enhance the savory and exquisite taste of lobster meat.
Use French thyme rather than English thyme; it has smaller leaves, is less bitter than the latter variety, and is closer to wild thyme because of its mixed aroma of verbena and lemon. You may even be able to find lemon thyme for sale in specialty produce markets. From ancient times, it has been credited with a thousand virtues: The Egyptians used it to embalm mummies, the Greeks consecrated it to the nymphs and the Romans used it both as a medicinal plant and as a flavoring. Today, if we have overindulged ourselves, it can help restore some color to our cheeks.
To give the sauce still more character, add a squeeze of lemon juice.
Cut the lobsters in two lengthwise before they are cooked, while they are still alive. Serve them hot, accompanied by saffron rice garnished with tomato pieces. Saffron goes very well with all seafood.
This dish is an excellent ambassador for business dinners, and would be a splendid addition to any Christmas or New Year's party. Since we are talking about parties, our wine expert suggests opening a bottle of one of France's most marvelous wines, a Puligny-Montrachet.

3. *Break open the pincers using a hammer.*

4. *Place the lobster halves in a baking dish and place little knobs of butter on each.*

Lemon Thyme Sauce

5. Sprinkle a little salt and pepper on the lobsters, and bake them in a very hot oven for about 15 minutes.

6. Let the rest of the butter soften, then blend in the lemon thyme, chopped parsley and lemon juice. Remove the lobsters from the oven. Spread the butter over the lobsters, return them to the oven for another 10 minutes, and serve.

Red Mullet with

1. Cut out the artichoke hearts with a knife. Rub each heart with lemon so that it does not turn brown.

Ingredients:
- 4 red mullets, 12¼ oz/ 350 g each
- 4 artichokes
- 1 lemon
- 1 tomato
- 6½ tbsp/100 ml olive oil
- 6½ tbsp/100 ml white wine
- 4 green olives
- 15 black olives

Serves 4
Preparation time: 30 minutes
Cooking time: 35 minutes
Difficulty: ★

2. Cut each artichoke heart into 8 pieces and remove the choke. Rub the pieces with lemon.

This recipe is childishly simple. The only difficulty is filleting the fish, but a fish retailer can do that for you. Do ask her or him to leave the skin on the fillets, as the pink color forms an integral part of the beauty of this dish.
Quick and easy, this exquisite recipe is perfect for clever people who do not have much time to spend cooking, but at the same time have no desire to renounce culinary pleasures. In a few minutes you will have put together an elegant dish that is quite original. It requires very little time spent in the kitchen, but a great result is guaranteed. Slices of sole fillet cut on the slant will also work marvelously with this recipe, redolent with flavors of southern France.
When the artichokes have been cut and cleaned, set them aside in water with lemon juice added so they do not turn brown. Remember that the artichoke is a vegetable that builds up health, and is recommended in the case of liver deficiencies and intestinal infections. Our wine expert suggests a Bellet Blanc from the Nice area, an excellent proof, if one were really necessary, that Provence produces more than just rosé!

3. Place a saucepan with salted water over heat. Add the pieces of artichoke. Skin, seed and finely chop the tomato and set it aside.

4. Add the juice of half a lemon to the artichokes and simmer over gentle heat. When the artichokes are tender, drain them.

Olives and Artichokes

5. Scale the red mullets and fillet them (see basic recipe), leaving the skin on. Grease the bottom of a frying pan and pour the olive oil and white wine into it. Salt lightly, add pepper and cook over gentle heat.

6. Arrange the red mullet fillets on a plate along with the artichoke hearts, and place the green and black olives on top of them. Garnish with the fresh tomato and parsley. Reduce the liquid in which the fish cooked, pour it onto the serving platter, and serve very hot.

Turbot Studded

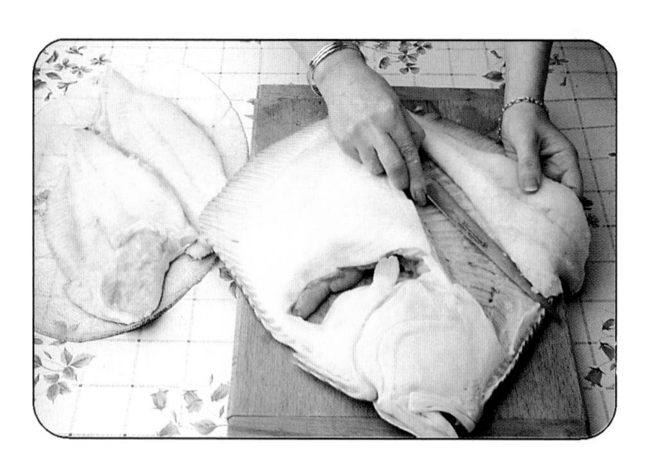

1. Fillet the turbot (see basic recipe).

Ingredients:
1 turbot weighing 4 lb 6 oz/2 kg
1 can of anchovies in oil
1 glass white wine
10½ oz/300 g salicornia
10 tbsp/150 g butter
2 tbsp salmon caviar
1 sprig of parsley
1 bunch of chives
salt and pepper

Serves 4
Preparation time: 35 minutes
Cooking time: 25 minutes
Difficulty: ★ ★

2. Cut the anchovies into small pieces. Use a small knife to make holes in the fillets and push the pieces of anchovy into them.

Salicornia is a delicious green seaweed that does not grow in the depths of the sea, but closer to the surface amongst the pebbles. The ebb and flow, and the movement of water with the tides, is indispensable for its well-being.
Here, the taste of turbot is enhanced by that of anchovies. This is delicious and a reminder of ancient times, when this method was used to salt meat and fish. Lamb, beef or veal could also be prepared in this time-honored manner.
You do not need to put salt on the fish: The anchovies will do that for you.
To make this dish even more magnificent for an extra-special occasion, consider studding the turbot not with anchovies, but with fine truffles, and making a champagne sauce for it as well.
The turbot is a highly regarded fish. The recipe our chef has created for it is simple but noble, one worthy of being served to guests of distinction.
Our wine expert suggests a Meursault Genevrières, a fine white Burgundy, inimitable with its roasted hazelnut aroma.

3. Place the fillets in a buttered frying pan. Add the white wine and pepper, but no salt, and cook for about 10 minutes over gentle heat.

4. Bring a saucepan of water to a boil, add salt, and poach the salicornia. Drain, let cool, and then sauté in 1 tbsp butter. Put aside.

with Anchovies

5. Blend the remaining butter with 3 anchovy fillets to make anchovy butter.

6. Reduce the cooking liquid from the turbots by half, then whisk the anchovy butter into it. Garnish with chives and parsley and serve very hot accompanied by salmon caviar and salicornia sautéed in butter.

John Dory in

1. Chop the leek, celery, onion and shallot. Sauté all the vegetables in a saucepan with some of the butter. Fillet the John Dory (see basic recipe).

Ingredients:
1 John Dory weighing 3 lb 4 oz/1.5 kg
1 leek
1 rib of celery
1 onion
1 shallot
5 tbsp/70 g butter
1 small bouquet garni
2 bay leaves
1 cup/250 ml white wine
1 lb/500 g potato purée
2 cups/300 g small young peas
⅔ cup/150 ml heavy cream
salt and pepper

Serves 4
Preparation time: 20 minutes
Cooking time: 30 minutes
Difficulty: ★

2. When the vegetables are cooked, add the head and bones of the fish together with the bouquet garni and bay leaves. Continue to sauté, then pour in the white wine and 2 cups/500 ml water. Salt lightly and simmer for 20 minutes.

This intriguing and visually apealling recipe can be prepared with a wide variety of white-fleshed fish, like brill or turbot, as well as the John Dory chosen by our chef.
If you let your fish retailer fillet the John Dory, remember to ask for the head and bones, which are needed to make the stock. Bones from river fish or those that have dark flesh should be avoided, as they can make a stock bitter.
Our chef would like to draw attention to the fact that the John Dory fillets should be poached very rapidly, rather than fried or baked.
Before making the pea cream sauce, put aside some of the peas to be used as garnish. Peas contain phosphorus, iron, potassium, the vitamins A and C, and carbohydrates. In season, fresh peas are a sweet treat for the tastebuds. The play of colors, white and green, will be prettily punctuated by their presence.
Connoisseurs will surely be able to appreciate this dish. Try a Château-Smith-Haut-Lafitte (Graves Blanc). The peppery characteristics of this wine give it plenty of charm.

3. Strain this fish stock through a fine sieve, then poach the John Dory fillets in it for 3 minutes. Set aside.

4. Combine half of the potato purée with 1⅓ cups/200 g of the peas. Adjust the seasoning.

Pea Cream Sauce

5. Reduce the stock in which the John Dory fillets cooked by half. Bring the heavy cream just to a boil and add the reduced fish stock to it. Simmer for several minutes.

6. Add the rest of the peas to this sauce, season with salt and pepper, and blend while adding the rest of the butter. Arrange the fish fillets on a serving platter and use a pastry bag to garnish with the 2 purées. Serve very hot.

Seafood Turbans

1. *Clean the salmon and monkfish fillets thoroughly, and then cut 4 strips from each. Put them aside.*

Ingredients:
1 salmon fillet, about 14 oz/400 g
1 monkfish fillet, about 14 oz/400 g
2 shallots
10 tbsp/150 g butter
¼ tsp saffron
1 cup/250 ml white wine
1 tbsp heavy cream
7 oz/200 g salicornia
salt and pepper

Serves 4
Preparation time: 25 minutes
Cooking time: 20 minutes
Difficulty: ✰ ✰

2. *Finely chop the shallots and sauté them in a little butter. Add the saffron and the white wine and reduce the mixture.*

This elegantly presented dish, in which red and white fish are cleverly braided together, already seduces with its appearance. The skillful mixture of aromas will also dazzle guests and make a huge impression on them. The colors are most important in this recipe. Salmon trout can substitute for salmon; it also has pink flesh. You can also replace the monkfish with any other fish with firm white flesh, like conger eel or turbot. Choose long-bodied fish so that you can cut strips that are easy to twist together.
This recipe will demand a little patience and dexterity, but the final creation is of such splendor that you will be amply compensated for your efforts.
Saffron perfectly enhances all seafood flavors, and its coloring will highlight that of the fish "turbans."
Salicornia, also called "sea bean," is harvested in mid-July. Do not add salt to the water it is cooked in, as seaweed is already quite salty.
Make holes in the tartlet molds used to cook the turbans to allow the liquid that is exuded during cooking to run into the sauce. Seafood Turbans with Salicornia deserves to be served at your most important meals. It will not fail to astound admiring guests.
Our wine expert suggests a Pouilly-Fumé (Ladoucette). The fruity aromas of this white wine surprise with their freshness in salmon dishes.

3. *Stir the cream into the shallots and wine and simmer for a few seconds.*

4. *Whisk the butter into this mixture, season with a little salt and pepper, then strain through a fine sieve. Set the sauce aside.*

with Salicornia

5. Braid together one strip of salmon and one strip of monkfish, and place the "turban" in a tartlet mold. Repeat with all the slices of fish. Sprinkle on a little salt and pepper.

6. Place the molds in a couscous kettle or steamer and cook the "turbans" for about 5 minutes. Poach the salicornia in unsalted water. Bring the sauce briefly to a boil once more. Pour it onto a serving platter, place the fish turbans in it, and accompany with salicornia. Serve very hot.

Eel Matelote

1. *Skin, trim, and gut the eels, then cut them into lengths. Dice the bacon and the mushrooms.*

Ingredients:
4 lb/1.8 kg eel
3½ oz/100 g bacon
7 oz/200 g button mushrooms
6½ tbsp/100 ml oil
3½ tbsp/50 ml wine lees or Chinon
1 carrot
1 lb/500 g potatoes
12 scallions
12 vineyard snails
3 cloves garlic
½ glass Cognac
2 veal stock cubes
13 tbsp/200 g butter
3 sprigs parsley
salt and white pepper

Serves 4
Preparation time: 45 minutes
Cooking time: 40 minutes
Difficulty: ✯ ✯

2. *Fry the pieces of eel in a frying pan with some oil. Season with salt and pepper. Blanch the bacon and sauté the mushrooms in butter.*

Cravant-les-Coteaux is an enchanting village on the Loire, and its vineyards use the respected trade name Chinon. The wine lees, or sediments, are used to make the marc produced in the hills above the Loire. It is not available commercially; one has to know a vintner in the region to obtain it. If you do not have this opportunity, a good Chinon will still be in keeping with this recipe and work just as well.

Skinning an eel is not a pleasant task, and is best done by a specialist, probably a fish retailer, who has the necessary skill for this delicate operation. Cutting the inside of each piece facilitates the cooking process without damaging the fish. The pieces of eel should be purged in water for quite a while.

Our chef offers a secret for cooking eel: Sear it over high heat, then remove it from heat and let it stand for 15 minutes before finishing it over gentle heat. Eel may have a higher or lower fat content depending on the season. Let the fat melt away during the second stage of cooking.

Do not forget to season the mushrooms during cooking: salt helps reduce their bitterness. In season, black grapes that have been peeled and seeded can be added to the sauce for a deliciously unexpected flavor.

Follow the golden rule and serve the wine used to flavor the sauce; in this case offer your guests a wine from Cravant-les-Coteaux.

3. *Peel and shape the carrots, potatoes and scallions. Poach them in separate saucepans of salted water.*

4. *Sauté the vineyard snails in a frying pan with a little butter; season with salt and pepper. Add the bacon, mushrooms, scallions and carrots. Cook, covered, over low heat and then set aside.*

with Chinon Wine

5. Reduce the wine lees, or the Chinon, in a saucepan. Add the crushed garlic, the Cognac and the veal stock cubes dissolved in 1¼ cups/300 ml water. Lightly salt and pepper and reduce by half.

6. Strain this mixture through a fine sieve, adjust the seasoning, and whisk in the remaining butter. Arrange the pieces of eel on the serving platter along with the vegetables, bacon and vineyard snails. Pour the sauce over everything, garnish with parsley and serve very hot with boiled potatoes.

Crumbed Pollack

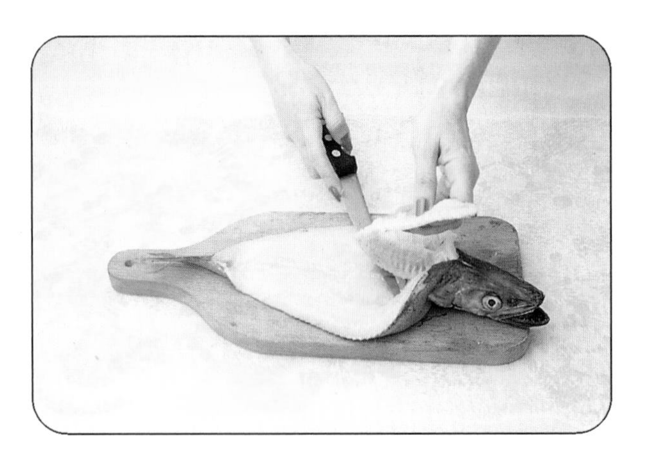

1. Trim and gut the pollack, and clean them thoroughly. Remove the central backbone (see basic recipe).

Ingredients:
4 young pollack, 400 g/14 oz
8 small carrots
4 pieces of broccoli
1 cauliflower
1 bunch of young turnips
4 scallions
1 tomato
1 celery heart
6½ tbsp/100 g butter
scant 3 cups/200 g fresh bread crumbs
2 lemons
2 sprigs parsley
salt and pepper

Serves 4
Preparation time: 45 minutes
Cooking time: 20 minutes
Difficulty: ★ ★

2. Select, clean and prepare the vegetables. Wash them thoroughly.

If possible, use pollack that have not yet reached adulthood for this recipe, as they are particularly delicious.

In order not to damage the flesh of the fish when removing the backbone, cut the parts connected to the tail and the head with scissors. You should also remove the black skin under the head, as this is rather unaesthetic.

Wrap the head and tail of the fish in aluminum foil to prevent them from burning when you put them under the grill.

Just before serving, if you like, coat the serving platter with a little veal gravy. This final touch will enhance the flavor of the whole.

Crumbed Pollack with Garden Vegetables combines flavors from the sea with those of several fresh, almost sweet, vegetables and offers a wide range of tastes to the delight of your guests.

Our wine expert suggests a Pouilly-sur-Loire. These wines, produced from the Chasselas grape variety, are remarkably balanced.

3. Lightly salt the vegetables, then steam, leaving them slightly crisp.

4. Pour a little oil into a roasting pan and dip the pollack in it, coating them on both sides. Sprinkle with salt and pepper.

with Garden Vegetables

5. Dip the pollack in the bread crumbs so they are well-coated. Clarify the butter. Place the fish on the roasting pan and drizzle with a little clarified butter.

6. Wrap the heads and tails of the pollack in aluminum foil. Squeeze a lemon over the fish and cook over high heat for about 15 minutes, or grill in the oven. Serve very hot accompanied by the vegetables.

Pike Scallops

1. Peel and chop the shallots. Fry them in a saucepan with 1 tbsp butter. Pour in the white wine and reduce until the moisture has evaporated.

Ingredients:
1 pike, about 2 lb 3oz/1 kg
4 shallots
6½ tbsp/100 g butter
1 glass white wine
1¼ cups/300 ml crème fraîche
7 branches stinging nettles
salt and pepper

Serves 4
Preparation time: 20 minutes
Cooking time: 30 minutes
Difficulty: ★

2. Fillet the pike (see basic recipe) and remove the skin. Cut the fillets in 2 pieces and cook them in a non-stick frying pan without oil. Add a little salt and pepper.

How bounteous is nature! Even when it punishes us, it has balsam ready to soothe our wounds. Nettles may sting, it is true, but properly prepared, they also give us their fresh green flavor. An herbaceous plant with stinging hairs, its edible leaves contain vitamins A and C. It contains more iron than spinach and is cooked exactly like it. It can be replaced by spinach—but why deprive yourself of the fun of gathering it? Nettles grow everywhere and can be found from March through November. Immerse them in boiling water to make them lose their sting.

Use the nettles to tame the ferocious pike with its 700 teeth; it will forget its aggressivity and become all tenderness and gentleness! Make sure the fish is fresh: most importantly, the gills should be red and glossy. Avoid pike with yellow skin on their belly. The pike can be replaced by other fish, but its rustic flavor combines so well with that of the stinging nettles that it would be a shame to do so.

Pike Scallops with Nettles should be served hot. The sauce can be reheated before adding the butter, but after the butter is added it tends to curdle.

If the nettles have convinced you of their value, you can accompany the pike with little nettle flans. Refer to the basic recipe for vegetable flans for guidelines.

This simple, quick recipe will provide you with a delicious meal for every day. For our wine expert, a fine dish deserves a fine wine; open up a Meursault Les Charmes.

3. Mix the crème fraîche with the shallots and bring to a boil over medium heat.

4. Blanch the nettle leaves in a saucepan of salted water. Drain and allow to cool.

with Nettles

5. When they have cooled, purée the nettles in a food processor and add to the sauce.

6. Bring the sauce to a boil. Strain it through a sieve, then whisk in the remaining butter. Adjust the seasoning. Pour the hot sauce over the serving platter and place the fillets in it just before serving.

Hogfish

1. Remove the outer layer of skin from 10 of the shallots and blanch them in a saucepan. Leave them to cool.

Ingredients:
15 shallots
10 tbsp/150 g butter
4 tsp/20 g sugar
4 hogfish fillets
1 lemon
salt and pepper

Serves 4
Preparation time: 25 minutes
Cooking time: 35 minutes
Difficulty: ★ ★

The hogfish is an inhabitant of warm and temperate waters, and in France it is caught along the Mediterranean coast. Its enormous head and pieces of loose skin hanging from its eyelids, have earned it monikers such as "devil," "toad" or "sea scorpion." Its dorsal fin bristles with venomous spines. The hogfish is rich in protein, and has a high content of phosphorus and magnesium.
If hogfish is hard to find, you can replace it by some other seawater fish.
Make sure the shallots are only cooked until they turn slightly brown and, to give the butter sauce a little more bite, squeeze some lemon juice on them.
To honor such a "devilish" fish, the chef recommends shallot flans as accompaniment.
Quick and simple, Hogfish with Shallots can be used as a hot appetizer as well. It should not be reheated under any circumstances, however. This is a dish to savor with friends so you can share the scary thrills provided by this marine monster in a pleasant atmosphere.
Our wine expert advises you to choose a fruity wine, as the sweetness of the shallots would be the cruel downfall of an acidic wine. Select a Pouilly-Fumé.

2. Sauté the blanched shallots briefly in butter. Sprinkle with salt and the sugar. Caramelize them for 10 to 15 minutes over medium heat.

3. Salt and pepper the hogfish fillets. Cook them in a non-stick frying pan without oil.

4. Peel and finely chop the rest of the shallots.

with Shallots

5. Clarify the rest of the butter, removing the milk solids. Heat the clarified butter, add the chopped shallots and cook until slightly brown.

6. Arrange the hogfish fillets on a serving platter and squeeze a lemon over them. Pour over the shallot butter sauce. Serve accompanied by a shallot flan and caramelized shallots.

Red Mullet

1. After washing the leeks thoroughly, cut them into julienne. Open the 4 oysters.

Ingredients:
4 red mullet, each
 1 lb 4 oz/ 600 g
4 leeks
4 oysters
13 tbsp/200 g
 unsalted butter
2 shallots
2 bay leaves
½ glass white wine
6½ tbsp/100 ml
 crème fraîche
2 tbsp/30 g
 coarse salt
salt and pepper

Serves 4
Preparation time: 20 minutes
Cooking time: 25 minutes
Difficulty: ★

2. Cook the leeks in a saucepan with 3½ tbsp/50 g butter. Salt very lightly and stir occasionly so that they do not brown.

The secret of this marvellous recipe lies in the unexpected taste of the oysters, which one discovers without seeing them. The crunchiness of the large grains of salt is also a refined and tasty surprise. This recipe can be varied on other occasions by replacing the leek with finely minced fennel, under which you can hide a quarter of an orange. This fruity treat should be served cold.
Red mullet, which is rich in protein and phosphorus as well as iodine, is suitable for children. If you cannot obtain red mullet, gilthead can also be used in this recipe.
Our chef advises you not to reduce the shallots completely, but to always leave a little wine—this will prevent the sauce from curdling. To thicken the sauce, whisk in small pieces of very cold butter.
Red Mullet with Leek Compote should be served very hot immediately after cooking. It will keep for one or two days in the refrigerator and can then be reheated in a microwave oven. To make the meal less rich, simply leave out the butter. It will then be perfectly suitable for slimming diets.
Our wine expert recommends the gentle lightness of a Graves blanc for this dish. Often neglected, the refinement of this underrated wine will do honor to your table.

3. Chop the shallots finely and sauté them in butter. Add the bay leaves and white wine and reduce the mixture by a quarter.

4. Stir in the crème fraîche and reduce briefly until the sauce thickens.

with Leek Compote

5. Add the butter to the cream sauce, whisk vigorously and adjust the seasoning if necessary. Bring briefly to a boil and put aside.

6. Steam the red mullet fillets. Poach the oysters briefly. Cover the bottom of a plate with the sauce, place the oysters in it and cover them with the red mullet fillets, placing a pinch of coarse salt on top. Form small mounds of leek and serve.

Salmon Trout

1. Fillet the salmon trout (see basic recipe) and set it aside. Clean the bones and head thoroughly and chop them. Chop the onion and leek and sauté in the oil. Add the fish bones, salt and pepper. Cover with water. Add the bouquet garni and simmer.

Ingredients:
1 salmon trout,
2 lb 10 oz/1.2 kg
12 oysters
1 onion
1 leek
2 tbsp oil
1 bouquet garni
1 bunch parsley
1 bunch chives
1 bunch tarragon
1 bunch cress
⅔ cup/150 ml
heavy cream
10 tbsp/150 g butter
salt and pepper

Serves 4
Preparation time: 35 minutes
Cooking time: 25 minutes
Difficulty: ★ ★

2. Open the oysters. Cut the trout fillets in two, then cut these pieces open lengthwise.

Crépinettes are a delicious French sausage traditionally made with pork, veal or other meats. In this case, the "sausages" are filled with a delightful blend of salmon trout, oysters, leeks and herbs.

In France, the salmon trout lives in the rivers along the coast of the English Channel and comes down to the sea before going back up the rivers in autumn. It is not always readily available. In this case you can use salmon, which some people even prefer for its richer and more compact flesh.

Trout drys out during cooking, so leave it on the stove only as long as necessary. The oysters should be warmed, but here, too care is required: If cooked for too long, they become rubbery.

The sauce should be prepared just before serving: If it stands too long, it can lose its color. Rice, either wild or white, is a good accompaniment which will not drown the distinctive taste of the cress sauce, but accentuate it.

Serve Salmon Trout Crépinettes hot; they cannot be reheated. This lovely dish, a mixture of flavors from the sea and the garden, makes for a light and elegant meal. Our wine expert suggests a Jurançon Moelleux (Clos Uroulat).

3. Salt and pepper the inside of the fillets. Finely chop the parsley, chives and tarragon. Place an oyster in the middle of a slice of trout and coat it with the herbs. Repeat with all the salmon trout.

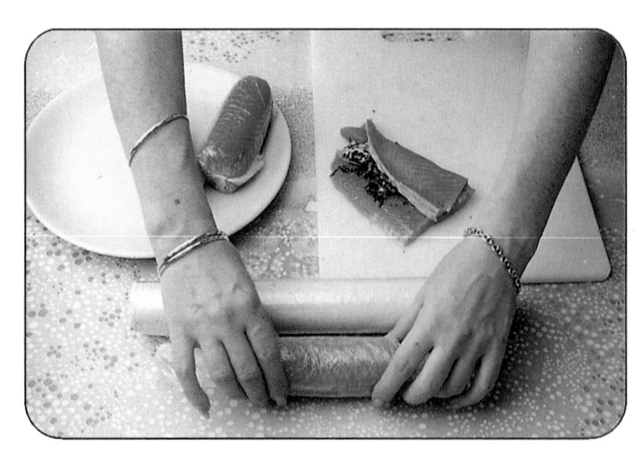

4. Roll up the trout fillets and wrap each "crépinette" in a piece of heat-proof plastic wrap, tying up both ends.

Crépinettes

5. Place the crépinettes in a baking dish and strain the fish stock from Step 1 over them. Place in a medium oven for about 10 minutes. Wash the cress thoroughly.

6. Pour half the liquid from the baking dish into a saucepan and reduce by half. Add the cream and let the sauce thicken. When ready to serve, add the cress, blend the sauce and adjust the seasoning. Whip the butter into the sauce, pour over the serving platter, place the crépinettes in it and serve right away.

Grouper Scallops

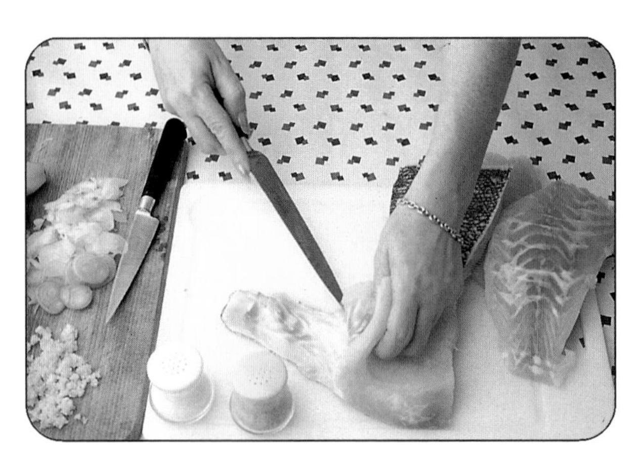

1. *If necessary, fillet the grouper and remove the skin (see basic recipe). Peel and mince the garlic and shallots.*

Ingredients:
1 grouper weighing
2 lb 3 oz/1 kg
2 cloves garlic
3½ oz/100 g shallots
10 tbsp/150 g butter
3½ tbsp/50 ml good quality vinegar
⅔ cup/150 ml red wine
12 anchovies
1 bouquet garni
1 bunch chives
1 bunch tarragon
1 bunch chervil
flour
salt and pepper

Serves 4
Preparation time: 15 minutes
Cooking time: 30 minutes
Difficulty: ★

2. *Fry the shallots in a saucepan with a little butter, then deglaze the pan with the vinegar.*

Despite its enormous head full of teeth, the grouper is a peaceable fish that inhabits warm waters, including the Mediterranean. Its meat is excellent, but it is rarely found in fish shops. If you cannot obtain it, hake can be used for this recipe.

The grouper has firm flesh that is easy to handle. Ask your fish retailer to fillet the fish and remove the skin for you.

Canned anchovies are much too salty for this recipe. Instead, use anchovies from Collioure and soak them to remove the excess saltiness.

Use a high-quality vinegar so that the shallots do not take on the taste of alcohol. The shallots should not brown, or the sauce will become bitter. The chef recommends chopping them with a knife, as they tend to lose their juice if this is done in a food processor. Reduce the vinegar until it has evaporated, then add a good red wine.

People for whom you have prepared Grouper Scallops with Anchovy Sauce will talk about your culinary talents for a long while afterwards. It should be served hot, accompanied by spinach, and cannot be reheated as it loses its firm texture.

This is a typical regional dish. Wherever you are, it will transport you to the Côte Vermeille. Our wine experts recommends a no-nonsense, vigorous wine, grown on sandy earth: a Listel blanc (Sauvignon).

3. *Pour in the red wine. Season with salt and pepper and cook for about 10 minutes over low heat.*

4. *Add the anchovies, garlic and the bouquet garni, and remove the sauce from the heat.*

in Anchovies

5. Chop up all the herbs and put them aside. Heat a little butter in a frying pan. Flour the grouper scallops and fry them in the butter. Season with salt and pepper.

6. Strain the sauce through a fine sieve and bring it to a boil. Whisk in the rest of the butter, then add the herbs. Cover the bottom of a serving platter with the sauce and place the grouper scallops in it. Serve hot.

Gamba Tails

1. *Cut the ham into small cubes and fry it in a saucepan with some olive oil. Add the chopped onion and continue to cook. Dice the mushrooms and shrimp.*

Ingredients:
12 gamba tails
3½ oz/100 g shelled shrimp
3½ oz/100 g raw ham
6½ tbsp/100 ml olive oil
1 onion
7 oz/200 g button mushrooms
1 cup/200 g uncooked rice
1 bouquet garni
2 packets of cuttlefish ink
1 fish bouillon cube
3 zucchini
12 mint leaves
24 toothpicks
salt and pepper

Serves 4
Preparation time: 40 minutes
Cooking time: 40 minutes
Difficulty: ★ ★

2. *Mix in the shrimp and mushrooms. Remove the tails from the gambas and shell them. Cut them in half and set aside.*

Exotic-sounding cuttlefish ink is regularly available at Catalan fish retailers. If the one near you, exiled far from those beautiful shores, cannot provide you with it, perhaps it can be ordered for you. The ink colors the rice but, surprisingly enough, does not change its taste. Instead, small pieces of shrimp, ham, mushroom, onions and garlic give the rice a wonderful flavor.
You can replace the gambas with langoustines, and the mint by a sprig of lemon balm, if desired. A salad with lemon dressing will complement this simple meal well.
The chef suggests a variation that he personally likes very much, serving the shrimp tails with couscous instead of rice. Rice can be easily reheated in a microwave oven, but the filled zucchini tend to become limp.
Serve Gamba Tails with Black Rice hot and have a feast. This original manner of preparing rice will be immediately appreciated by your family, and you will have a great success. Surprise your guests by serving a wine from Hérault: a Mas de Daumas-Gassac.

3. *Add the rice and bouquet garni to the mushroom mixture. Season with salt and pepper and stir.*

4. *Thoroughly mix in the cuttlefish ink. Dissolve the stock cube in 1¼ cups/300 ml water and pour onto the rice. Add more water as needed while cooking over gentle heat.*

with Black Rice

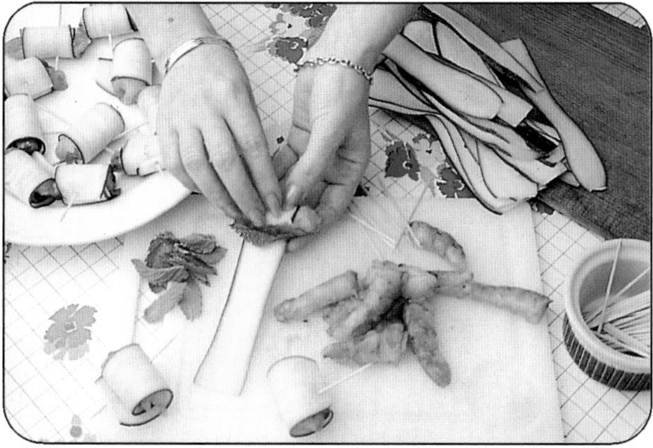

5. Cut the zucchini lengthwise into thin strips. Wrap each piece of gamba tail in a strip of zucchini along with a mint leaf. Hold the rolls together with a toothpick.

6. Salt and pepper the gamba rolls and cook them in a pan with olive oil. Once the rice is done, arrange it in a crown shape on the serving platter. Place the rolls around it and accompany with beurre blanc (see basic recipe). Serve very hot.

John Dory Picadas

1. Peel and cube the potatoes and cook them in lightly salted water.

Ingredients:
1 John Dory,
2 lb 10 oz/1.2 kg
14 oz/400 g potatoes
1¾ oz/50 g black olives
1¾ oz/50 g green olives
1 slice of white bread
1 pinch saffron
1 pinch cayenne pepper
1 pinch slivered almonds
4 mint leaves
olive oil
1 cup/250 ml beef stock (see basic recipe) or 1 bouillon cube
peanut oil
2 tbsp flour
salt and pepper

Serves 4
Preparation time: 25 minutes
Cooking time: 35 minutes
Difficulty: ★ ★

2. Pit the olives and chop them into small pieces. Fillet the John Dory (see basic recipe) and put it aside.

The John Dory is one of the great seawater fish. It has white, firm flesh that comes away from the bone easily and lends itself to several methods of preparation. You can also use turbot or any fish with tender meat, even cod.
John Dory is easy to manage, so your dish is sure to succeed. Its succulence results from it being cooked *à la meunière*, which means "in butter."
This recipe, typical of the Catalan region, has been adapted to modern tastes for your pleasure. Using chicken stock or gravy from a roast made the night before instead of a normal stock cube. will make the sauce particularly flavorful, and adding olive oil will make a delicous potato mousseline out of any sort of potato. The sauce contains neither flour nor cream and is bound only by the bread crumbs and almonds. And as you will see, it works marvellously!
John Dory Picadas with Potato Mousseline is certainly a recipe to add to your list of culinary gems. It should be served immediately after cooking.
Dare to be original and serve a Mercurey blanc (Marquis de Jouennes).

3. Remove the crusts from the bread and cut it into small pieces. In a food processor, combine the bread cubes, saffron, cayenne pepper, slivered almonds and the mint leaves. Blend to form a paste, adding a little olive oil if necessary.

4. Mash the potatoes. Stir in the chopped olives and a little olive oil. Adjust the seasoning if necessary.

with Potato Mousseline

5. Dissolve the bouillon cube in 1 cup/250 ml water and bring it to a boil. Bind the sauce with the seasoned bread and almond mixture. Adjust the seasoning if necessary and set it aside.

6. Heat a little peanut oil and butter in a frying pan. Flour, salt and pepper the John Dory fillets, then fry them. Cover the serving platter with the sauce. Place the fish fillets on it accompanied by the potato mousseline with olives, and serve hot.

Perch Gâteau

1. Peel and finely chop the onions. Cut the tomatoes in half, seed and finely dice them. Fillet the perch (see basic recipe) and put them aside.

Ingredients:
2 perch
8¾ oz/250 g onions
2 cloves of garlic
6 tomatoes
1 cup/250 g butter
1 lb 9 oz/750 g potatoes
1 bouquet garni
1 bouillon cube
juice of 1 lemon
6½ tbsp/100 ml olive oil
salt and pepper

Serves 6
Preparation time: 40 minutes
Cooking time: 1 hour
Difficulty: ★

2. Sauté the onions and tomatoes in separate saucepans with a little butter. Add the garlic to the tomatoes.

In the green and pleasant valley of the Dordogne, streams full of delicious fish abound. The perch is one of them, with which you are doubtless acquainted. A close relative of the walleye, it also lives in lakes and is cooked in the same fashion.

Our chef recommends the white perch, which has tender and easily digestible flesh. It is low in fat, rich in phosphorus, and has a subtle, refined flavor. Like all freshwater fish, perch has many bones, so when filleting the fish, use tweezers to carefully remove them. Other possibilities in this recipe might be the flathead catfish or walleye, if there is a fisher about, or use a saltwater fish with tender flesh that does not dry out, like the turbot or the John Dory.

Potatoes *à la boulangère*, a mixture of potatoes and onions, is a culinary classic. The novelty in the present recipe is that a galette is made from potatoes, and the superb perch is placed royally in the middle. Do not use too much water when cooking the potatoes. They should not be covered so that the top becomes nice and crusty.

Perch Gâteau à la Boulangère is very easy to make. The seasoning is important; use the various herbs and spices to give the potatoes flavor. Serve this refined and high quality dish very hot and enjoy.

Our wine expert recommends a Saint-Aubin Blanc to introduce you to this little village in Burgundy that produces marvelously fruity wines.

3. Peel and thinly slice the potatoes. Place a layer of onions and a layer of potatoes in the bottom of a large saucepan. Repeat until all the potatoes and onions have been used. Season with salt and pepper.

4. Place a bouquet garni on top of the potatoes and onions, pour in the bouillon cube dissolved in a glass of water and cook for about 30 minutes in a medium oven.

à la Boulangère

5. Make a vegetable vinaigrette out of the sautéed tomatoes, lemon juice and olive oil. Season with salt and pepper. Thoroughly grease a cake pan and cover the bottom with attractive slices of the potatoes to form a rosette. Press it down well.

6. Place the perch fillets on this rosette. Fill the cake pan with the rest of the potatoes and onions, sprinkle with a little water and bake in a moderate oven for about 20 minutes. Serve hot, accompanied by the tomato vinaigrette.

Sole and Scallop

1. Peel and finely chop the shallots. Fillet the sole (see basic recipe), flatten each fillet slightly and cut into long strips. Wrap a scallop in each one and put aside.

Ingredients:
2 sole
16 scallops
2 shallots
3 tbsp butter
2 tbsp/30 ml
white wine
1 lb/500 g fresh
chanterelle
mushrooms
2⅓ cups/600 ml
crème fraîche
1 bunch of chervil
salt and pepper

Serves 4
Preparation time: 35 minutes
Cooking time: 30 minutes
Difficulty: ★

2. Sauté the shallots briefly in a pan with 1 tbsp butter, then add the bones from the sole, the wine and a little water. Salt lightly, add pepper and simmer.

The combination of scallops and fish used here is rich in potassium and iodine, low in calories, excellent for your health and provides a wonderful light meal. The best time for scallops is between October and March, making this a recipe to brighten up chilly autumns and gray winters.

The sole and scallops are steamed. Remember that the cooking time should be short, since scallops quickly become rubbery if overcooked, so pay attention to it, the only difficulty in this otherwise simple dish. If you do not have a steamer, the roulades can be poached in fish stock.

The sole can be replaced by any flatfish at all, such as lemon sole. The fillets have to be thin enough to wrap around the scallops.

Sole and Scallop Roulades with Chanterelles, rich in trace elements, goes very well with green vegetables. Broad beans will also be delicious with it. Serve hot and enjoy it right away, as this dish should not be reheated.

Elegance and refinement being the dominant elements in this meal, a Meursault is the inevitable choice of our wine expert.

3. Salt and pepper the roulades and steam them.

4. Sauté the chanterelles in a pan with the remaining butter. Season with salt and pepper. Stir occasionally.

Roulades with Chanterelles

5. Once the fish stock from Step 2 has reduced by half, stir in the crème fraîche, cook for several minutes, then strain into a saucepan.

6. Finely chop a handful of chanterelles and add them to the sauce. Cook briefly, adjust the seasoning and serve the roulades and the chanterelles with this sauce. Garnish the plate with chervil leaves.

Salmon Trout

1. *Peel and finely chop the shallots; mince the mushrooms in a food processor. Sauté half the shallots in a saucepan with 1 tbsp butter. Once they are golden brown, add the mushrooms.*

Ingredients:
1 salmon trout, about 2 lb 3 oz/1 kg
4 cups/1 liter mussels
5¼ oz/150 g clams
5 shallots
1 lb/500 g button mushrooms
6½ tbsp/100 g butter
¾ cup/200 ml white wine
2⅔ cups/600 ml crème fraîche
salt and pepper

Serves 4
Preparation time: 30 minutes
Cooking time: 30 minutes
Difficulty: ★ ★

2. *Fillet the salmon trout (see basic recipe) and cut the fillets into 4 slices. Steam the mussels and clams in the white wine just until they open; retain the liquid. Shell the mussels and clams and coarsley chop them.*

Duxelles is a forcemeat made from button mushrooms, onions and shallots sautéed in butter. Our chef has transformed them for this recipe, and makes his duxelles from finely chopped mussels and clams.
A fish retailer can certainly fillet and skin the salmon trout for you, but you will stive have to use tweezers to patiently remove the small bones.
Do not reduce the liquid from the mussels too much, or the sauce may become overly salty. Serve the fish very hot and eat immediately, as it is not suitable for reheating.
Keeping to the theme of mixing fish and shellfish, you can create many variations using salmon, cockles and oysters, for example. The palette offered by the depths of the sea allows infinite variations. Lovers of fish and seafood will appreciate this refined dish, one that will enchant the palate. It is very rich in potassium and phosphorus, which will stimulate your creative intellect.
Our wine expert suggests a Bandol Rosé.

3. *Now add the mussels and clams to the mushroom duxelles. Salt lightly, add pepper if necessary, and simmer over gentle heat.*

4. *Stir in ¾ cup/200 ml of the crème fraîche and cook another 5 to 6 minutes.*

in Shellfish Duxelles

5. Let this mixture cool, then spread it on the salmon trout slices and poach them briefly in the liquid in which the shellfish were steamed.

6. Strain the cooking liquid through a fine sieve or paper filter to eliminate all the grains of sand. Reduce it by ¾ and then add the rest of the crème fraîche. Vigorously whisk in the remaining butter, adjust the seasoning and serve this sauce as an accompaniment to the fish.

Scallop Galette

1. *Thoroughly wash the lettuce. Blanch it in salted water for 5 minutes, then refresh it in iced water.*

Ingredients:
12 scallops
1 head of lettuce
1 lemon
¾ cup/180 g butter
oil
1 sprig of flat-leaf parsley
salt and pepper

Serves 3
Preparation time: 15 minutes
Cooking time: 20 minutes
Difficulty: ★

2. *Finely chop the lettuce. Squeeze the lemon and reserve the juice.*

Scallops are very popular in France, where they are the most-eaten shellfish after oysters and mussels. They are enjoyed because of their taste, and have always been admired for their elegant, harmonious form and fine ribbing. They are very common on the coasts of Galicia in Spain, and are traditionally served to pilgrims making the journey to Santiago di Compostela.

Before sautéing the lettuce in butter, squeeze it in absorbent paper to make it as dry as possible. Do not be surprised at the quantity of butter required to cook the lettuce: It will absorb it all without leaving any over. This also acts as an indication: When all the butter has disappeared, the lettuce is ready.

Cooking the coral from the shellfish is a very rapid process, which should be done overy very gentle heat. It does not take more than a few seconds and requires all your attention. So that this delicate, small, orange, moon-shaped coral does not burst, prick it gently with a pin.

To give your galette a perfect shape, just as if you had traced it with a compass, use a circular mold when arranging the lettuce and scallops.

Scallop Galette with Lettuce is a superb light meal, exquisitely elegant and delicious. The floral aromas of a Château Fieuzal (Graves Blanc) are astonishingly refined. Our wine expert wholeheartedly recommends it.

3. *Sauté the lettuce in a saucepan with ⅓ cup/80 g butter. Season with salt and pepper and put it aside.*

4. *In a non-stick pan containing a little oil, sear the scallops on both sides.*

with Lettuce

5. Pour the lemon juice into a saucepan and bring it to a boil. Season with salt and pepper, whisk in the rest of the butter and set it aside.

6. Arrange the lettuce on a serving plate. Cut the scallops into thin, round slices and place them on the lettuce to form a spiral. Drizzle the melted butter with lemon juice around the rim of the plate, garnish with parsley and serve.

Osso Buco

1. Clean and trim the pollack and cut it into steaks. Salt and dredge the steaks in flour. Peel and finely chop 1 carrot, 1 shallot, 1 clove of garlic and 1 rib of celery. Skin, seed and dice the tomato. Cut the zest of the lemon and orange into very thin pieces.

Ingredients:
2 lb 3 oz/1 kg pollack
flour
3½ oz/100 g carrots
2 shallots
1¾ oz/50 g celery stalks
1 clove of garlic
1 tomato
1 lemon
1 orange
6½ tbsp/100 ml
white wine
1 onion
1 bouquet garni
butter
1 tbsp tomato paste
parsley
salt, white pepper

Serves 4
Preparation time: 40 minutes
Cooking time: 45 minutes
Difficulty: ✯ ✯

2. Pour ¾ of the wine and some water into a saucepan. Add the rest of the carrots, the onion, bouquet garni and the leftover fish and simmer. Strain through a sieve and reduce until you have 2 cups/500 ml of stock.

In Italian, *ossobuco* (or *osso buco*) means "bone (with) hole" in Italian. The traditional Italian dish is a ragoût made from veal knuckles braised in olive oil and white wine with onion, tomato and other flavors.
Taking this as a starting point, our chef has had some fun recreating it, but this time without bones, having chosen fish as the main ingredient. It is just one step from the land to the sea, but one has to be inspired to take that step in the first place. Those who love surprises, the unexpected and transformations can only be delighted by this boldness. Our chef has otherwise kept to the original Italian recipe.
Cut round steaks of pollack towards the tail so that they resemble veal fillets. Cooking the pollack will require all your attention: If the fish is cooked too long, it will fall apart. The sauce should not be too thick. If you dip a spoon into the sauce and it coats the curved side, the consistency is right.
Osso Buco with Pollack should be served hot. It will keep for one or two days, but fish are better freshly cooked. Inexpensive and simple, it is perfect for reunions with friends. Our wine expert recommends a Saint-Roman Rouge. This vintage from the Beaune region is still a little timid, but will soon have a very good reputation.

3. Sear the pollack steaks in a frying pan with a little butter. Put them aside. Heat a little more butter in the pan and add the mirepoix of celery, carrot, shallot and the garlic. Mix in the lemon and orange zest and cook over gentle heat.

4. Pour the rest of the white wine into the pan. Add a little salt and pepper.

with Pollack

5. Add the pieces of tomato, the reduced fish stock from Step 2 and the tomato paste, and simmer for a few moments.

6. Place the pollack steaks in the sauce and simmer for about 3 minutes. Arrange the steaks on a serving platter. Whisk butter (amount to taste) into the sauce and pour over the fish steaks. Garnish with parsley and serve hot.

Skate in Steamed

1. *Pour the olive oil into a baking dish and add the lemon juice, thyme leaves, bay leaf and crushed coriander seeds. Fillet the skate if necessary (see basic recipe). Remove the skin and place the fillets in the marinade. Cover the dish and refrigerate.*

Ingredients:
4 portions of skate
olive oil
juice of 1 lemon
fresh thyme
bay leaf
½ tsp coriander seeds, crushed
4 large savoy cabbage leaves
6½ tbsp/100 ml vinaigrette
1¾ oz/50 g finely chopped herbs (basil, parsley, tarragon, chervil)
1 fish stock cube
salt and pepper

Serves 4
Preparation time: 20 minutes
Marinating time: 24 hours
Cooking time: 25 minutes
Difficulty: ★ ★

Undressed, plunged into a perfumed bath, and decorated with greenery: Could a skate dream of more voluptuous treatment?
To begin, remove the thick skin from the portions of skate. The simplest thing is to ask the fish retailer to do it along with the filleting. If you do choose to do it yourself, use a razor-sharp knife.
The skate is marinated for 24 hours to let it become impregnated with all the flavorings. After placing it in the marinade, turn it over, then cover with plastic wrap before refrigerating it. The next day, there will be no need to spend much time in the kitchen: The cooking times are very short.
This recipe is also good with freshwater fish, perhaps walleye or pike fillets.
Served hot in its delicate green wrap, Skate in Steamed Cabbage Leaves will bring the simple elegance of all great recipes, and the refinement of light cuisine, to your table.
Vinaigrette sauce and herbs tend to drown the taste of wines. Your choice should therefore be a rich wine with a touch of acidity. Our wine expert suggests a Saint-Véran.

2. *Pull apart the cabbage. Remove the stems and blanch the leaves, then drain and let cool.*

3. *Place a cabbage leaf on a chopping board. Drain a skate fillet and wrap it in the leaf. Make sure it is completely enclosed. Repeat with all the fillets.*

4. *Steam the cabbage rolls for about 15 minutes and salt them lightly.*

Cabbage Leaves

5. Combine the vinaigrette and finely chopped herbs in a food processor and blend.

6. Dissolve the stock cube in 6½ tbsp/100 ml water, reduce it slightly to yield approximately ¼ cup/60 ml, and add to the vinaigrette. Mix thoroughly. Pour the vinaigrette onto the serving platter. Place the rolls in the sauce and serve.

Trout

1. *Peel the carrots and the onion.*

Ingredients:
2 live trout
3½ oz/100 g carrots
1 small onion
1 bouquet garni
a few coriander seeds
2 whole cloves
zest of 1 orange
zest of 1 lemon
potatoes
salt and pepper

Serves 2
Preparation time: 10 minutes
Cooking time: 20 minutes
Difficulty: ★

2. *Slice the carrots and gut the trout.*

Some very particular gourmets, and there are many of them, are of the opinion that, of all known ways of cooking trout, Trout au Bleu is the only one worthy of consideration. Jean Giono, who was regarded as a great connoisseur in this field, wrote: "Never cook it with butter, never cook it with almonds, that is all just pretence … Apart from Trout au Bleu, there is no other method of cooking trout." For gourmets with a taste for quality, this recipe is an essential proof of good taste.

For the meal to succeed perfectly you need river trout, small wild trout that have been freshly caught. Of course, this presupposes a happy, fruitful fishing expedition. Otherwise, live farmed trout are the next best thing.

Trout au Bleu is very easy to prepare, requiring only a rapid execution.

Pour generous amounts of vinegar over the trout after gutting it and see how it displays all its iridescent colors: an impressive sight!

Trout au Bleu can also be accompanied by hollandaise sauce. With its refined flavor, this light dish will certainly give you and your guests much gastronomic pleasure.

The Jurançon Sec is a true friend of trout, and is the best choice to accompany this dish.

3. *Cut the onion into rounds, then separate the rings.*

4. *Cook the vegetables and seasonings in a saucepan with water: carrots, onion, bouquet garni, coriander and cloves, orange and lemon zest. Add salt and pepper and simmer for 20 minutes.*

au Bleu

5. *After gutting the trout, pour vinegar over them so that they take on a slightly blue color. Cut the potatoes into pear-shaped pieces and cook them in a saucepan with salted water.*

6. *Immerse the trout in the vegetable stock, simmer for 5 minutes, and serve accompanied by the vegetables and small boiled potatoes.*

Salmon Quoits

1. Fillet the fish (see basic recipe). Cut 4 small slices of salmon and 4 small slices of John Dory and set them aside. Purée the rest of the flesh in a food processor.

Ingredients:
1 salmon fillet
1 John Dory
3½ tbsp/50 g butter
4 eggs
6½ tbsp/100 ml
crème fraîche
2 carrots
1 onion
2 cloves of garlic
2 cups/500 ml
red wine
2 bay leaves
1 sprig of thyme
3½ tbsp/50 g
beurre manié (see glossary)
salt and pepper

Serves 4
Preparation time: 40 minutes
Cooking time: 45 minutes
Difficulty: ⭑ ⭑

2. Add the butter to the fish purée and blend.

For this game of gastronomic hopscotch, invite friends who enjoy playing, or childhood companions who will appreciate that you have given the fish the appearance of those flat, square pebbles that give so many children pleasure.
Wrap the fish tightly in the plastic wrap so that you can remove the "quoits," or pucks, without difficulty.
To make the sauce satiny smooth, add a dollop of butter by swirling the saucepan until it barely melts just before pouring the sauce over the fish.
This dish can be accompanied by soft roe or fried roe, both of them a delight. Small mushrooms as well as croutons grilled with butter can be added. Give them different shapes to add to the visual pleasure.
In this recipe the fish is braised in red wine, a method that is called by the glorious name *chambord* in French cuisine. Salmon Quoits à la Chambord will give social gatherings a welcome element of surprise and sparkle.
Our wine expert recommends a Champagne Veuve Cliquot Rosé.

3. Break in the eggs and mix, then blend in the crème fraîche and some salt and pepper.

4. Spread out a piece of plastic wrap and place 1 slice of John Dory, 1 tbsp fish mousse and 1 slice of salmon on it, sandwiching the fish together with the mousse. Wrap the "quoit" in plastic wrap.

à la Chambord

5. Peel and finely chop the carrots, onion and garlic. Brown them with the fish bones. Flambé the red wine, then pour it in. Add the bay leaves, sprig of thyme, salt and pepper. Reduce for about 20 minutes, then strain through a fine sieve.

6. Bring this liquid to a boil once more and reduce it briefly. Adjust the seasoning and gently whisk in the beurre manié. Steam the "quoits." Cover the serving platter with the sauce, remove the plastic wrap and place the "quoits" on the serving platter. Serve hot.

Salmon

1. In a pan, glaze the pearl onions in ½ tbsp butter, sugar, a pinch of salt and a little water. Remove the rind from the bacon and chop; cut the bacon in thin strips. In a large pot, add 4 cups/1 liter water to the lentils.

Ingredients:
1 lb 11 oz/800 g smoked salmon, unsliced
3½ oz/100 g slab bacon
1 lb/500 g French lentils
1 bouquet garni
1 onion
2 whole cloves
2 bay leaves
1 handful pearl onions
3½ tbsp/50 g butter
1 tbsp superfine sugar
⅔ cup/150 ml crème fraîche
3 tbsp grated horseradish
salt

Serves 4
Preparation time: 25 minutes
Cooking time: 50 minutes
Difficulty: ★

2. Add the bouquet garni, pieces of bacon fat, bay leaves and the onion studded with cloves, and simmer until the lentils are tender. Blanch the strips of bacon briefly in boiling water, then fry them in a pan with 1 tbsp butter.

Cloves, which were introduced to Europe in about the fourth century, were for a long time as popular as pepper. In the past they have been highly regarded both for their culinary and medicinal uses.
The effect of cloves used in association with onion is very fortuitous: Cooking them together brings out the sweetness of the onion while mellowing the cloves' pungency.
Lentils, rich in carbohydrates, iron and calcium, are very nutritious and easy to digest. The water used to cook the lentils should only be salted toward the end of the cooking period, since salt slows the cooking process.
The pieces of bacon need only be poached for a few seconds in salted boiling water. The fat rind is also cut into pieces and added to the stewing lentils to lend them the smoky flavor of the bacon.
For variety, you can also make this recipe using haddock.
The presence of the salmon make this meal unexpectedly fine, and it is sure to enchant the whole family.
Our wine expert recommends an Alsatian Tokay du Domaine F.- E. Trimbach.

3. Stir the pearl onions occasionally to ensure they brown well.

4. Bring the crème fraîche to a boil, then add the grated horseradish. Salt lightly and reduce briefly.

with Bacon

5. Whisk butter into the horseradish mixture, bring it briefly to a boil, adjust the seasoning and put aside.

6. Remove the skin from the salmon, slice the flesh, and fry it gently in butter. Make sure it stays tender. Place the lentils in a serving dish and arrange the salmon, bacon strips and glazed onions on top. Coat with the horseradish sauce. Serve very hot, or cold accompanied by a little vinegar.

Trout

1. *Scale and trim the trout.*

Ingredients:
4 trout weighing
10½ oz/300 g each
flour
1 cup/250 g butter
3½ oz/100 g slivered
almonds
1 lemon
chervil
salt and pepper

Serves 4
Preparation time: 20 minutes
Cooking time: 20 minutes
Difficulty: ★

2. *Gut the trout (see basic recipe).*

People who have the good fortune to live in Brittany, or in a region where there are lakes and rivers, will certainly prefer to use wild trout (salmo trutta fario) in this recipe. Its flesh has a firmer consistency, and is less dry and easier to work with, than the traditional rainbow trout, or farmed trout. It has a subtle hazelnut taste and those who have had the pleasure find it most flavorful.
If there are avid anglers among your friends, promise them to prepare this dish if they bring you a basket of brook trout.
You can also use a saltwater fish. This recipe works very well with sole, for example.
Trout with Almonds is a festive dish, light and elegant. The crunchiness of the almonds is a treat. The trout are enough in themselves and do not require an accompaniment.
Our wine expert recommends a Pouilly-Fuissé (M.Vincent). This wine breathes nature, fishing, and joy! This is the occasions to benefit from it!

3. *Sprinkle salt and pepper on the trout and flour them.*

4. *Heat a little of the butter (⅓-¼) in a frying pan and fry the trout.*

with Almonds

5. Melt the rest of the butter in a separate frying pan. Add the almonds and brown them over gentle heat, stirring occasionally.

6. Place the trout on a serving platter and cover them with the almonds and butter. Drizzle lemon juice over them. Garnish with chervil leaves and serve very hot.

Breton Lobster

1. *Bring a large pot of water to a boil and place the lobsters in it for 5 minutes.*

Ingredients:
2 lobsters, each
1 lb 4 oz/600 g
oil
⅔ cup/150 ml whisky
3 cups/750 ml
heavy cream
6½ tbsp/100 g butter
cayenne pepper
salt and pepper

Serves 4
Preparation time: 10 minutes
Cooking time: 20 minutes
Difficulty: ★

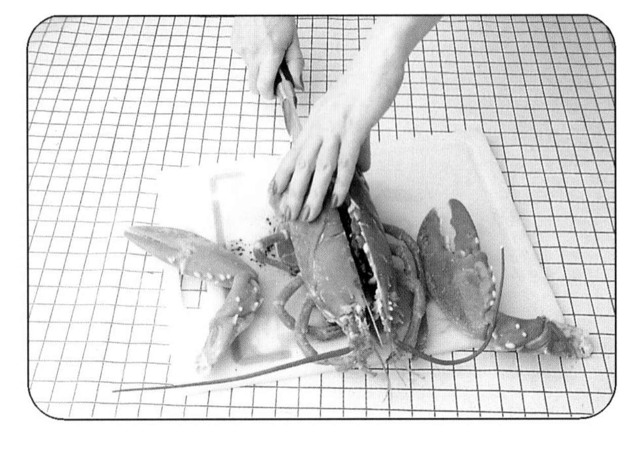

2. *Cut the lobsters in two (see text).*

Lobster enjoys such prestige that its presence on the menu almost always signifies some grand occasion. It used to be quite abundant in France along the coast of Brittany, which explains why there is a particular manner of preparing it typical of the region. Indeed, it is difficult to walk about this coastal area without yielding to the pleasure of trying a noble lobster bathed in whisky.

Cutting the lobster in two requires a vigorous and resolute approach. Lay it on its tail, with the tail flat, and insert the blade of a strong knife at the point that separates the line dividing the head in two. Start cutting toward the tail, then turn the lobster and finish with the head.

Creole rice is a festive accompaniment for this royally red crustacean.

When you have strained the sauce through a sieve, adjust the seasoning to taste, pour it over the lobster and serve very hot. This dish, one with a fine tradition, makes for exceptional dinners; it is a great event in itself.

Our wine expert recommends opening a fine bottle of Puligny-Montrachet.

3. *Pour some oil into an oven-proof frying pan and sear the lobster halves, meat side down.*

4. *Turn the lobsters when they are golden brown and flambé them with ¾ of the whisky. Season lightly with salt and pepper.*

Flambéed in Whisky

5. Pour in the heavy cream. Lightly salt and pepper, then bake in a moderate oven for 10 minutes.

6. Place the lobsters on a serving platter and pour the cream into a saucepan. Reduce over gentle heat. Add cayenne and adjust the seasoning, then blend the rest of the whisky into the sauce. Simmer again for a few minutes. Pour over the lobsters and serve very hot.

Belon Oysters

1. Peel and finely chop the garlic and shallots; chop the parsley as well.

Ingredients:
3 dozen
belon oysters
2 cloves garlic
3 shallots
1¼ oz/50 g parsley
1 cup/250 g
soft butter
3½ oz/100 g
slivered almonds
salt and pepper

Serves 6
Preparation time: 25 minutes
Cooking time: 10 minutes
Difficulty: ★

2. Add the garlic, shallots and parsley to the softened butter and blend well.

Perhaps you have heard of belon oysters, named after a small river situated about 7 miles from Pont-Aven. They are small and flat, with grayish-white flesh and an iodised flavor. If you cannot find belon oysters, or would like some variation, this recipe is also suitable for clams amd mussels.

Do not be afraid to add salt. Although the oysters are already salty, the blandness of the almonds needs to be compensated for when seasoning. On the other hand, do not overdo the garlic. It should not overly dominate or it will ruin the delicate flavor of the filling.

This recipe does not present any difficulties. Take care, however, when browning the almonds under the grill, as they do not need long at all.

Arrange the oysters on a bed of seaweed or coarse salt to keep the shells stable and make an attractive presentation. A true Bretonne would use the delicately-flavored coarse grey salt from the salt marsh of Guérande, formerly one of the most valuable products of Brittany. A softer bed of salicornia, a green plant related to algae, is also possible.

Our wine expert suggests a fine wine from the Beaune region: a Chevalier-Montrachet. It is extremely rare, but if you have the chance to procure it, you should not hesitate an instant. Its golden-green coloring and lemon bouquet will bewitch you.

3. Season with salt and pepper, mix thoroughly, and set the herbed butter aside.

4. Open the oysters carefully and detach the flesh from the wall of the shell.

with Almonds

5. Discard the liquid from the oysters and coat them with the seasoned butter.

6. Sprinkle the oysters with sliced almonds and grill them for some minutes just before serving.

Squid and Sweet

1. Prick the sweet red peppers with a fork, grill them well over a gas flame, then scratch off the entire skin with a knife. Wash them under running water and put them aside.

Ingredients:
4 squid weighing 7 oz/200 g each
6 sweet red peppers
1 onion
2 leeks
2 cloves of garlic
5¼ oz/150 g button mushrooms
1 tomato
1¼ cups/300 ml olive oil
cuttlefish with ink
2 cups/500 ml fish stock (see basic recipe)
beurre manié (see glossary)
1 bunch of chervil
salt and pepper

Serves 4
Preparation time: 45 minutes
Cooking time: 35 minutes
Difficulty: ✯ ✯

2. Peel the onion, wash the leeks, and finely chop both. In a little butter sauté the onions, then add the leeks. Finely dice 2 of the peppers. Sauté them with the garlic and add to the onions and leeks. Cut the mushrooms and tomato into small pieces.

Our chef is enthusiastically loquacious about this recipe. He compares this "vice versa" to the magical transition from negative to positive with the development of a photo. Here you are introduced to the secrets of the darkroom.

The best way to peel the peppers is to grill them until the skin has turned black and brittle. Then rub off the skin under running water; it will come off easily.

The order of cooking the vegetables is important: first lightly sauté the onions, then the leeks until they are soft and tender, and finally the mushrooms.

Both cuttlefish and squid, also called calamari, are full of water and may jump about in the frying pan. They should not be allowed to shrink too much.

It can be difficult to obtain ink in packets, but squids always contain some, and that will be enough to make the sauce. This operation is a messy one and it is best to ask your fish retailer to recover the ink for you.

Serve this meal hot. If you have Basque or Spanish guests, they will be very touched by this friendly gesture. All your guests will be satisfied, and you can be sure that they will not leave anything on the plate. That is just as well, because you should not reheat this dish. Our wine expert recommends a Châteauneuf-du-Pape (Château de Beaucastel). This generous and bracing wine will tame the exuberant flavor of the sweet pepper.

3. Sauté the whole peppers over gentle heat in a saucepan with olive oil. When they are cooked but still slightly crisp, set aside. Fry the squid that you will be stuffing, complete with the heads, then put them aside.

4. Cut the cuttlefish into small pieces and fry it in another pan. Reserve the ink. Add the button mushrooms and chopped tomato to the sautéing vegetables from Step 2. When ready, stir the cuttlefish into this stuffing mixture.

Red Peppers Vice Versa

5. For the dark sauce, reduce the fish stock and then mix in the cuttlefish ink. Reduce once more and add a little beurre manié. For the red pepper sauce, dice 2 peppers and cook in a little water until soft, then purée well in a food processor.

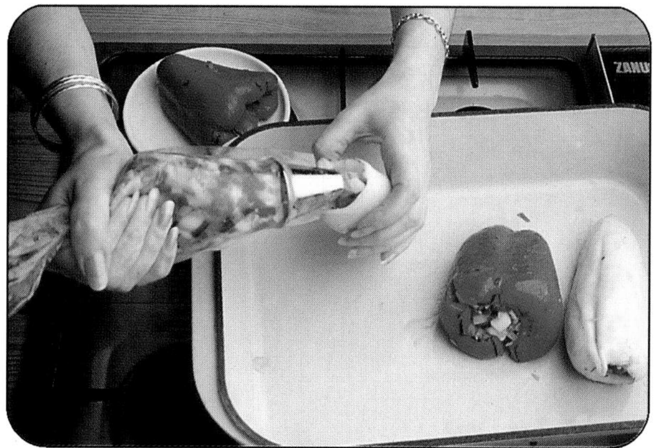

6. Use a pastry bag to fill the peppers and squid with stuffing. Lightly salt and pepper, then roast in the oven for several minutes. Nap one side of a serving platter with red pepper sauce and the other with dark sauce. Place a stuffed pepper on the ink sauce and a stuffed squid on the red sauce; garnish with chervil; serve hot.

Pollack with

1. *Cut up the veal trimmings and brown in a saucepan. Chop the onion, 1 carrot and 2 cloves of garlic, and add to the veal. Sauté without browning. Add the bouquet garni, chopped tomato, and salt and pepper, then cover with water and simmer over gentle heat.*

Ingredients:
1 pollack, about
1 lb 11 oz/ 800 g
veal trimmings
1 onion
3 carrots
1 head of garlic
1 bouquet garni
1 tomato
1 leek
ginger to taste
3 tbsp/45 g butter
¾ cup/200 ml
port wine
1 tbsp red currant
jelly
oil
salt and pepper

Serves 4
Preparation time: 40 minutes
Cooking time: 45 minutes
Difficulty: ★★

Sweet-and-sour dishes may seem exotic, but even medieval cuisine, having inherited the flavorings of ancient times, contained piquant and sweet-and-sour sauces. The novel idea of preparing pollack in this manner lends this otherwise serene fish a completely new level of passion.
Our chef recommends using very little oil, because the meat will give off enough fat. If veal trimmings are not available, use poultry, which will do the job just as well.
To keep the veal sauce clear, skim off the fat while it is cooking. It is simmered over very gentle heat, and it is best to do it a day in advance to save time. The vegetables should be sautéed very gently in butter, without browning. If you think you may not manage this, add a little water. The ginger should be added right at the end.
Ginger, celebrated as much for its therapeutic virtues as for its gastronomic qualities, will bring all its power to bear and neutralize the intense sugar from the red currant jelly. The secret of this sweet-and-sour sauce lies in this combination. It is invigorating and a great pleasure for the palate.
It is said that good Rieslings have a "kerosene" aroma! Uncork a bottle right away and all will become clear!

2. *Slice the leek and remaining 2 carrots into julienne. Finely chop the ginger. Sauté the carrots, leek and ginger in a covered saucepan with 1 tbsp butter. Add a little salt and pepper.*

3. *Pour the port wine into a saucepan. Flambé it, then reduce by half.*

4. *Strain 2 cups/500 ml of the veal stock made in Step 1 into the reduced port wine. Again reduce by half over gentle heat.*

Sweet-and-Sour Sauce

5. Add the spoonful of red currant jelly to the vegetable julienne. Whisk the rest of the butter into the sauce and adjust the seasoning.

6. Cut the pollack flesh into steaks and fry them in a pan with oil. Season with salt and pepper. Coat the serving platter with the sauce. Arrange the pollack on it and place a spoonful of the julienned vegetables on each steak. Serve hot.

Sole

1. *Fillet the sole (see basic recipe). Put aside 1 fillet, then knot the others and place them in a greased baking dish. Add salt and pepper and set aside. In a saucepan sauté half the chopped shallots, pour in half the white wine and steam the mussels in it.*

Ingredients:
2 sole
1 cup/¼ liter mussels
8 each: crayfish, oysters and langoustines
1 lobster claw
2 shallots, finely chopped
1 glass of white wine
cayenne pepper
1 cup/250 g butter
8 button mushrooms
flour
1 egg, lightly beaten
breadcrumbs
6½ tbsp/100 ml oil
2 cups/500 ml fish stock (see basic recipe)
juice of 1 lemon
4 slices of truffle
salt and pepper

Serves 4
Preparation time: 45 minutes
Cooking time: 35 minutes
Difficulty: ★ ★

2. *Bring a saucepan of salted water to a boil. Add a pinch of cayenne pepper and cook the crayfish. Open the oysters and poach the lobster claw in the water used for cooking the crayfish.*

Sole Normande enjoys a well-established reputation. This refined recipe, which combines the most typical products of Normandy, has become so popular that it is enjoyed everywhere. It is said that this manner of preparing the fish was invented by a Parisian chef in the 19th century, when it was made with cider and garnished with mussels, oysters, shrimp tails, mushrooms, truffles, gudgeons, crayfish and more.
This dish, part of a great tradition, runs the whole gamut of marine flavors—assuming, of course, that you retain the liquid in which the mussels and oysters are cooked and use it as the basis for the sauce.
The chef recommends clarifying the butter used for frying the prawns. The oysters should only be opened at the very last moment, just before cooking them. They should be just warmed, rather than cooked, or they will become rubbery.
This sole dish, sumptuously garnished, will enchant your seafood-loving friends. If Sole Normande is popular, it is often at the cost of its authenticity. Our chef's recipe initiates you into the secrets of the cuisine of his region, and it is a true delight.
Uncork a particularly fine bottle in honor of this grand classic dish: a Chassagne-Montrachet Blanc.

3. *Shell the langoustine tails, add salt and pepper and brown in a frying pan with a little clarified butter. Poach the mushroom caps.*

4. *Cut the reserved sole fillet in strips. Lightly salt and pepper, then roll the strips first in flour, then in the beaten egg, then in breadcrumbs. Fry them in a pan with a little oil.*

Normande

5. Sprinkle the rest of the chopped shallots over the knotted sole fillets. Strain the liquid from the mussels into the baking dish, add the rest of the white wine and the fish stock, and cook 15 minutes in a hot oven. Shell the mussels and put them aside. Shell the lobster claw.

6. Remove the sole fillets from the pan and reduce the liquid by half. Whisk the butter and lemon juice into this sauce and adjust the seasoning. Arrange the fish and the other seafood on a plate, cover with the sauce and garnish with mushroom caps and slices of truffle. Serve very hot.

Langoustines with

1. *Shell the langoustines and remove the intestines. Put 2 small leaves of sage inside each tail and wrap in a slice of bacon. Put aside.*

Ingredients:
20 langoustines
1 sprig of sage
20 small slices of bacon
2 tomatoes
7 oz/200 g lentils
1 bouquet garni
1 carrot
2 cloves of garlic
2 whole cloves
1 shallot
6½ tbsp/100 g butter
1 chicken stock cube
3½ tbsp/50 ml oil
salt and pepper

Serves 4
Preparation time: 35 minutes
Cooking time: 40 minutes
Difficulty: ★

2. *Skin, seed and crush the tomatoes. In a saucepan of water, simmer the lentils along with the bouquet garni, carrot and garlic cloves, one of them studded with the cloves. When the lentils are almost tender, add salt.*

Although it is obvious, one cannot stress enough how essential it is for the langoustines to be fresh. As you will probably not be able to obtain these crustaceans alive at your fish retailer, be careful which ones you choose. They should have a slightly transparent shell. If you see black points where the female carries its eggs, then it is not fresh.
If using slab bacon, our chef recommends that you place it in the freezer for an hour or so in order to make it easier to slice it thinly and evenly.
Oil is preferable to butter for cooking the langoustine tails, as butter can turn an unpleasant color unless clarified butter is used. Start by cooking the side of each roll which will be presented.
You will surprise all your guests with Langoustines with Bacon and Lentils, which is both delicious and elegant. It is not every day that one takes the risk of combining langoustines with lentils. Let yourself be tempted. Our wine expert warmly recommends a Pouilly-Fuissé (Georges Dubœuf) because of its mineral and vegetal aromas.

3. *Chop the shallot and brown it in a saucepan with a little butter. Once it becomes golden, add the crushed tomatoes.*

4. *Add the drained lentils to this mixture along with the diced carrot. Cover and simmer over low heat, and adjust the seasoning.*

Bacon and Lentils

5. Dissolve the bouillon cube in ¾ cup/200 ml water and reduce it by ¾. Fry the langoustine tails over gentle heat in a frying pan with a little oil.

6. Add the rest of the butter to the chicken stock and blend in a food processor. Cover a plate with the sauce, mound some lentils in the center, and surround with langoustine rolls. Serve very hot.

Whiting with Curry

1. *Peel the potatoes and boil them in salted water.*

Ingredients:
5 whiting fillets
1 lb/500 g potatoes
2 shallots
13 tbsp/200 g butter
1 tbsp curry
6½ tbsp/100 ml white wine
6½ tbsp/100 ml crème fraîche
1 bunch of sorrel
1 bunch of cress
juice 1 lemon
6½ tbsp/100 ml oil
salt and pepper

Serves 4
Preparation time: 20 minutes
Cooking time: 30 minutes
Difficulty: ★

2. *Peel and mince the shallots and sauté them in a saucepan with a little butter. Mix in the curry and continue to cook. Pour in the white wine.*

Whiting is a lean fish with tender, flaky meat that is not too costly, and can be obtained all year round. Its only drawback is that it tends to fall apart during cooking. To avoid this, our chef advises leaving the skin on and cooking the whiting on the side with the skin. The fillets must be handled with care, and there will still be some bones that need to be removed using tweezers.
Other fishes, like cod or turbot, are also suitable for this recipe.
Whatever fish you choose, it should be cooked in clarified butter or oil, rather than butter in its usual state, which tends to clacken when heated intensely.
For the accompaniment, the chef has had the marvelous idea of combining cress with a little sorrel. The flavor of the cress, normally quite mild, is brought out by this hint of acidity, and is revealed in all its serene power.
Whiting with Curry Sauce and Cress Purée demonstrates that it is entirely possible to make a dish with character using simple ingredients.
Our wine expert tells us that the Ladoix Blanc (Domaine C. Chevalier) is a vintage related to the fine Corton-Charlemagne, and feels this meal will be an excellent occasion to try it!

3. *Reduce the white wine almost completely, then whisk in 10 tbsp/150 g of the butter to form the sauce.*

4. *When the potatoes are cooked, drain them. Mash them with a fork, adding 3 tbsp/50 g butter and the crème fraîche.*

Sauce and Cress Purée

5. Blend the sorrel and the cress together with the lemon juice. Blend this mixture into the potatoes.

6. Slice the whiting fillets and fry them in a pan with some oil. Add a little salt and pepper. Bring the sauce to a boil and adjust the seasoning. Strain it through a fine sieve and pour over a serving platter. Arrange the whiting fillets on the platter interspersed with spoonfuls of the potato and cress mixture.

Skate with

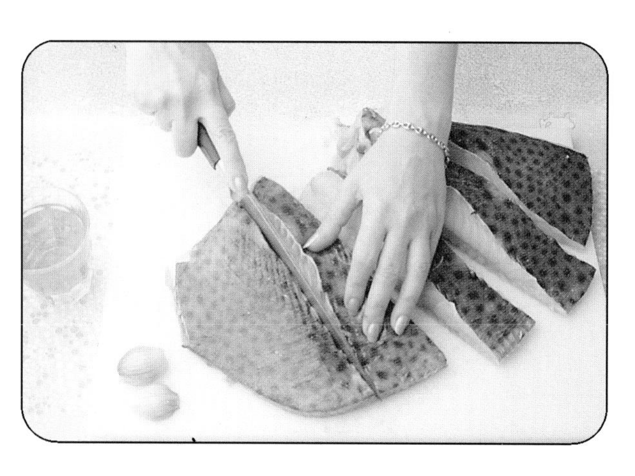

1. Cut the wing of the skate into 6 equal portions and wash them thoroughly.

Ingredients:
1 skate "wing"
2¾ oz/80 g shallots
1 packet powdered court-bouillon or other rich bouillon
13 tbsp/200 g butter
1⅔ cups/400 ml *vin jaune*
cayenne pepper
1 bunch of chervil
salt and pepper

Serves 4
Preparation time: 20 minutes
Cooking time: 25 minutes
Difficulty: ★

2. Peel and finely chop the shallots. Dissolve the court-bouillon or other bouillon in 6 cups/1.5 liters water, in a pan large enough to hold the fish.

Vin jaune, literally "yellow wine," is an original product of the Jura region which has its own appellation (*Appellation d'Origine Contrôlée*). It is a dry white wine of excellent quality with a sumptuous yellow color and a plum and nut aroma, a wine that will keep magnificently for a century or even two.

Using *vin jaune* in this recipe gives it a regional touch. Other white-fleshed fishes, such as the large-scaled scorpionfish or the cunner, could also be used if desired. To rid the skate of its ammonia odor, which is often quite strong, it must be purged in cold water for one or two hours.

Removing the thick, gelatinous skin of the skate is a delicate operation. It is easier to do this after the skate has been cooked.

Our chef recommends finishing the sauce by whipping in the well-chilled butter over very gentle heat, or even without heat. This will serve to thicken it and improve its flavor. Skate with Vin Jaune should be served very hot, accompanied by small pieces of boiled leek sautéed in butter, Creole rice or steamed potatoes.

Our wine expert recommends a Château-Chalon. This *vin jaune* is one of the ten finest French wines, and if you are not familiar with it, now is the perfect occasion—and one not to be missed—to try it.

3. Bring the court-bouillon to a boil and add the 6 pieces of skate. Simmer over gentle heat for about 15 minutes.

4. Sauté the shallots in a little butter. Add the vin jaune and reduce by ¾. Whisk in the rest of the butter, well-chilled and cut into small pieces.

Vin Jaune

5. Add a pinch of cayenne pepper and a little salt and pepper to the sauce. Place it in the top of a double boiler to keep it warm.

6. Remove the skin from the pieces of skate and arrange them on a serving platter. Cover them with the sauce and garnish with chervil. Serve very hot.

Crayfish

1. Peel and chop the shallots, carrots and leek. Cut the tomatoes in narrow wedges. Soak the morels in water. Wash the crayfish thoroughly and fry them in a saucepan with very hot oil.

Ingredients:
3 lb 4 oz/1.5 kg crayfish
3 shallots
2 carrots
1 leek
4 tomatoes
1¾ oz/50 g dried morels
3½ tbsp/50 ml oil
1 bouquet garni
3½ tbsp/50 ml Cognac
1 tbsp tomato paste
¾ cup/200 ml
white wine
¾ cup/200 ml
heavy cream
2 egg yolks
3½ tbsp/50 g butter
salt and pepper

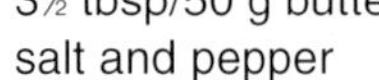

Serves 6
Preparation time: 40 minutes
Cooking time: 30 minutes
Difficulty: ★ ★

2. Add the shallots, leek, carrots and tomatoes to the crayfish, then the bouquet garni. Simmer.

Here is an old recipe from Lyons dating back to the time when the Rhone river abounded in crayfish, which were only eaten on feast days and at important celebrations. Today, there are scarcely any of these crustaceans to be found in this region, and locals have resigned themselves to eating crayfish imported from elsewhere to satisfy an appetite that has not changed.
Our chef insists that crayfish should only be cooked in season, that is, from the middle of August to the middle of December. Avoid eating them out of season.
Crayfish should not be cooked too long. As soon as they turn red, they are sufficiently done. They should be cooked in a covered pot, as the steam plays an important role. Crayfish with red claws are best.
This rich dish, with its simple beauty, will give a meal a sober and inimitable elegance. Take the advice of our wine expert and open a Puligny-Montrachet to honor the refinement of crayfish. Only a fine wine from the Beaune region can match it.

3. Pour the Cognac onto the crayfish and flambé it. Season with salt and pepper, stir in the tomato paste, and combine thoroughly.

4. Pour in the white wine and a glass of water water and cover the pot. Cook for about 10 minutes.

Gratin

5. Remove the crayfish from the liquid. Shell them and put them aside. Reduce the remaining liquid, then add the heavy cream and let the sauce thicken again.

6. Wash the morels thoroughly in several changes of water. Strain the sauce through a fine sieve into a saucepan, adjust the seasoning, and add the morels. Cover and simmer briefly, then whisk in the egg yolks and butter. Cover the crayfish with the sauce and glaze briefly under a grill.

Blanched Skate

1. Pour half of the white wine and some water into a roasting pan. Add the chopped carrot, onion, thyme, bay leaf, cloves, salt and pepper, and a sprig of chervil. Add 2 tbsp of the vinegar.

Ingredients:
2 lb 3 oz/1 kg skate
¾ cup/200 ml white wine
1 carrot, sliced
1 onion, chopped
thyme
bay leaf
2 whole cloves
1 bunch of chervil
6½ tbsp/100 ml white vinegar
1 pint raspberries
2 shallots
6½ tbsp/100 ml crème fraîche
13 tbsp/200 g butter
salt and pepper

Serves 4
Preparation time: 15 minutes
Cooking time: 30 minutes
Difficulty: ★

2. Cut the skate into pieces and poach it in this mixture.

In Lyon people enjoy eating skate, especially with *beurre noir*, or "black butter," a sauce based on butter that has been heated until it turns dark brown. It is certainly delicious, if not very good for the figure. Our chef's skate recipe, however, is both flavorful and low in calories.

Here is an effective method of removing the skin of the skate: If you immerse the skate in boiling water, the skin can be pulled off easily. The fish should then be cooked without the skin, because the skin would fall apart in the court-bouillon, spoiling the elegance of the dish. As skate alone can be a little bland, season the court-bouillon well and cover the skate generously with it.

If you wish to make your own raspberry vinegar, the best season is autumn. In September, these little red fruits are already at their height for flavor. Place the reddest possible raspberries in glass jars and cover them with white vinegar. You will be able to use the raspberries all year round; they need only be puréed. Raspberry vinegar can be found in all larger grocery stores.

Blanched Skate with Raspberry Vinegar is a tempting meal. Our chef has chosen sobriety, lightness and refined elegance as his themes, and you will be delighted to partake of such a feast.

Our wine expert recommends a Saint-Romain Blanc. Discover this lovely vintage from the Beaune region, close to the fine Meursault.

3. Pour the remaining vinegar over the raspberries and leave them to marinate.

4. Purée the raspberries and vinegar in a blender or food processor, then strain through a fine sieve to eliminate the seeds.

with Raspberry Vinegar

5. Peel and finely chop the shallots. In a saucepan, combine with the rest of the white wine and reduce until dry. Stir in the crème fraîche, let thicken over low heat, then whisk the butter into the sauce.

6. Arrange the pieces of skate on a serving platter. Strain the sauce through a fine sieve. Add salt, pepper and the raspberry-vinegar purée to the sauce, pour over the skate fillets, and serve hot.

Fisherman's Chaudreé

1. Fillet the sole and the skate (see basic recipe). Slice the cuttlefish into round pieces. Skin and gut the eel, and cut it into ¾-in/2-cm lengths.

Ingredients:
10½ oz/300 g sole fillet
10½ oz/300 g skate
10½ oz/300 g cuttlefish or squid (the white part)
10½ oz/300 g eel
2 onions
6½ tbsp/100 g butter
1 glass Muscadet
1 bouquet garni
2 cloves of garlic
4 large leaves of green cabbage
1 bunch of chervil
salt and pepper

Serves 4
Preparation time: 40 minutes
Cooking time: 30 minutes
Difficulty: ★

2. Peel and chop the onions. Sauté them in a saucepan with some butter. When they are golden brown, add the glass of Muscadet and 4 cups/1 liter water.

Chaudrée is the lovely French name for the contents of a *chaudière*, or cauldron. All along the coast of Vendée and Saintonge, a chaudrée is a fish stew made from sole, small skates, minuscule cuttlefish locally called *casserons*, sometimes with pieces of eel, and many other fish. This is all cooked in Muscadet with butter, thyme, bay leaf and a little garlic. The fish with firm flesh, like conger eel, are put into the saucepan first.
You will have guessed that the chaudrée is to Charentes and the Atlantic what bouillabaisse is to Marseille and the Mediterranean. However, this stew is not red, but white. Success is assured as long as you keep to the different cooking times and follow the instructions of the chef faithfully.
Serve it as soon as it is cooked … hot!
This winter dish will be excellent after an appetizer of mussels. The flavors of the sea will sing on your palate: Let yourself be lulled by this call of the sirens that will transport you to the open sea.
To enhance these oceanic flavors, our wine expert recommends the delicious iodine aroma of a Muscadet sur lie.

3. Cut all the fish bones into large pieces and add them to the onion mixture. Season with salt, pepper, the bouquet garni and garlic.

4. Blanch the cabbage leaves in a saucepan with salted water. Drain and cool, then set them aside.

with Cabbage

5. Use a hand mixer to blend the stock, then strain it through a fine sieve. Bring the liquid to a boil and reduce by a quarter.

6. Poach the fish in the stock. Add a little salt and pepper. Place some of each fish on a cabbage leaf. Serve very hot accompanied by the sauce, garnished with finely chopped chervil.

Filleting Fish

1. *Remove the fins. Open the fish along its back and run the knife down the backbone. Cut the fillet at the top, removing it from the head. Lift the whole fillet by running the knife along the side bones.*

Ingredients:
1 whole fish
knife

Time required: 10 minutes
Difficulty: ✯ ✯

2. *Turn the fish over and repeat.*

Removing fillets from a fish is a delicate operation.
Before you begin, make sure that your tools are appropriate to the task. The knife should be long, sharp, and flexible in order to glide along the bone.
The technique is the same for all fish, with the exception of particularly thin fish, such as sole, or particularly thick ones, such as tuna.
This is a precise operation that demands care. Follow the directions scrupulously to remove the bones without damaging the fillets.

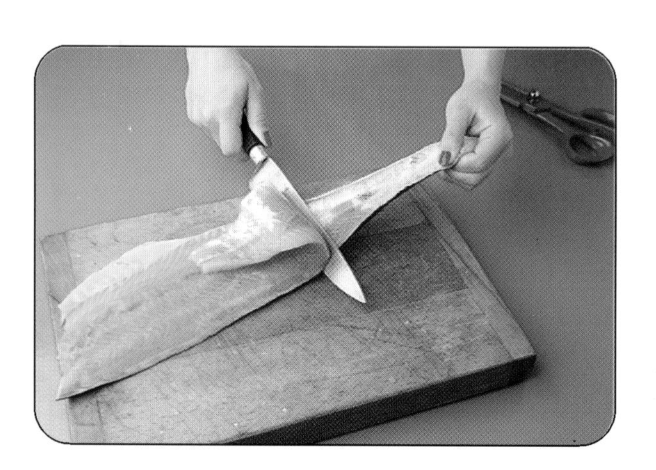

3. *Remove the skin by carefully sliding the knife between the skin and the flesh.*

Filleting Sole

1. *Remove the black skin from the sole. Turn it over and remove the white skin. Trim the fish with a pair of kitchen scissors.*

Ingredients:

1 sole or other flatfish
knife
scissors

Time required: 20 minutes
Difficulty: ☆ ☆

2. *Cut open the sole along the backbone using a pointed knife with a flexible blade. Slide the knife under the fillet, starting near the head and pressing against the backbone. Repeat with the second fillet on the first side. Trim the fillets to neaten their edges.*

Smaller flatfish like sole must be skinned before they can be filleted. You may wish to ask for this to be done when you purchase the fish. Use a knife with a long, pointed blade to fillet fish to ensure that the meat will not be torn in the process.

Unlike thicker fish, flatfish yield four fillets: one above and below the backbone on each side. To begin, carefully insert the knife between the upper end of the fillet (just at the base of the head) and the ventral bones. Lift the fillet slightly and separate it from the bone a little at a time while holding the fillet with your thumb. Once the fillet is detached near the head, it is quite easily separated from the bones along the entire length of the fish by sliding the knife along the backbone. Then simply cut the fillet from the tail and trim the edges.

Follow the same procedure for the second fillet. Then turn the fish over and remove the other two fillets. The bones and trimmings can, of course, be used to make a fish stock (see basic recipe).

3. *Turn over the sole and again cut along the central backbone. Repeat the procedure to detach the other 2 fillets. Beat the fillets to flatten them and break the nerves, then soak for 20 minutes in cold water. The sole fillets are now ready to use.*

Removing a Fish's Backbone

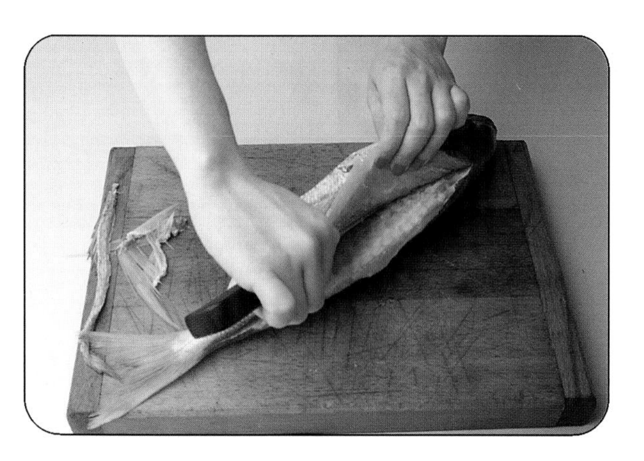

1. *Place the fish on a chopping board and trim it using the scissors. Open up the back of the gilthead by slicing along the backbone with the knife.*

Ingredients:
1 gilthead or other rounded fish
knife
scissors
tweezers

Time required: 10 minutes
Difficulty: ☆ ☆

2. *Repeat on the other side of the backbone.*

Many people like fish, but do not eat it because they have a horror of bones. This is a shame, because it is actually quite easy to "debone" a fish before cooking it.
The procedure may look complicated at first sight, but it really is not difficult. All it requires is a little concentration and dexterity. If you apply yourself, you will no doubt be able to successfully prepare whole fish in any way you like.
The technique shown here applies to rounded fish that you would like to serve whole. Follow our instructions very carefully.

3. *Cut the backbone away from the head and the tail with the scissors. Pull out the backbone, taking care not to tear holes in the fish. Use the tweezers to remove any small bones that are still in the flesh. The fish is then ready to prepare.*

Beurre Blanc (Beurre Nantais)

1. *Peel the shallots and chop them finely. Brown them in a saucepan in a little butter. Pour in the vinegar and white wine, then reduce over low heat.*

Ingredients:
3 shallots
3½ tbsp/50 ml vinegar
6½ tbsp/100 ml white wine
3 tbsp crème fraîche
1 cup/250 g butter
salt

Preparation time: 10 minutes
Cooking time: 10 minutes
Difficulty: ☆ ☆

2. *When the vinegar and wine have evaporated, add the crème fraiche. Stir and bring briefly to a boil.*

The simplest dishes can become elegant meals when they are accompanied by tasty sauces. In the case of this *beurre nantais*, which is a smooth and exquisite sauce that accompanies many dishes in the Angevin region and the area around Nantes, good quality butter will give the sauce a particularly subtle flavor. *Beurre nantais*, which is usually flavored with aromatic herbs such as fennel, parsley, chives or tarragon, lends a delicate savor to fish dishes, one recognised and appreciated by fine gourmets.
If you strain out the shallots, and add lemon juice and a little water while incorporating the butter, you will obtain a classic *beurre blanc*. *Beurre blanc* is more neutral than *beurre nantais*, which makes it an ideal accompaniment for dishes that require little seasoning.
In both cases, be sure that the butter is well-chilled when whisking it into the sauce or it will not thicken it properly. Whisk continuously to incorporate enough air to give your butter sauce a thick, yet light consistency.

3. *Cut the very cold butter into pieces, then add it gradually to the sauce while whisking constantly. Salt the sauce lightly. Strain it through a sieve to remove the shallots, if desired.*

White Stock

1. *Blanch the trimmings or giblets, starting with cold water. Bring to a boil, drain, refresh under cold water, and set aside. Peel the onions and garlic; stud the shallots with cloves. Split the leeks, and coarsely chop the carrots, celery, and onions. In a large pot, cover the vegetables with cold water and add the bouquet garni.*

Ingredients:

1 lb/500 g veal trimmings and/or poultry giblets
2 onions
2 cloves of garlic
1 shallot
4 whole cloves
2 leeks
2 carrots
1 celery stalk
1 bouquet garni
¾ cup/200 ml white wine
salt and peppercorns

Preparation time: 15 minutes
Cooking time: 1 hour
Difficulty: ✯

2. *Add the blanched veal to the vegetables, or if using poultry, add the vegetables to the blanched giblets. Season with salt, add the white wine and peppercorns, and simmer for about 40 minutes.*

A white stock base is made from poultry or veal. The process is slightly different if you are using poultry giblets: Begin by blanching them as described, always starting with cold water. Bring the water to a boil and skim off the foam frequently. When the foam disappears, instead of draining and refreshing, simply add the vegetables and seasonings to the giblets and continue to simmer for an additional 45 minutes.
Be sure to skim off any fat that appears while the stock is cooking, as the clarity and quality of the broth depends on this step.
If the broth will not be used immediately, you can store it in the freezer. Let it cool completely before pouring it into containers.

3. *When finished cooking, strain the stock through a fine sieve, and skim. It is ready to use.*

Lobster Bisque

1. Clean or peel and coarsley chop the vegetables; peel and dice the tomatoes. Separate the head and tail of the lobster. Split the head open and break the claws. Fry the lobster pieces in the very hot oil. Add the vegetables to the pot and brown briefly. Flambé the pan with the Cognac, then add the tomatoes.

Ingredients:
1 live 14-oz/400-g lobster
1 leek
1 onion
2 carrots
1 celery stalk
2 cloves of garlic
2 tomatoes
3½ tbsp/50 ml oil
3½ tbsp/50 ml Cognac
2 cups/500 ml fish stock or
1 cube bouillon
1 tbsp tomato paste
¾ cup/200 ml white wine
1 bouquet garni
whole cloves
¾ cup/200 ml crème fraîche
1 tbsp butter
1 tbsp flour
salt and peppercorns

Preparation time: 30 minutes
Cooking time: 35 minutes
Difficulty: ☆ ☆

2. Bring the fish stock to a boil. Stir in the tomato paste and white wine; season with salt and pepper. Add the bouquet garni and cloves and simmer briefly. Pour the stock into the pot with the lobster, and top off water to cover. Simmer for about 30 minutes. Blend the butter and flour to make a beurre manié.

3. Remove the lobster meat, strain the broth through a fine sieve, and stir in the beurre manié. Return to the heat, blend in the crème fraîche, and simmer until thickened. Adjust the seasoning and serve garnished with sliced lobster meat.

In current practice, "bisque" refers to a smooth, self-flavored sauce—traditionally a creamy broth of lobster, although scampi, crabs, crayfish, or any crustacean can successfully be used as the basis for this bisque.

Lobster bisque is refined, aristocratic fare suitable for festive occasions or for special guests able to appreciate gourmet presentations of high quality. It is likely to remain at the top of any first-rate menu for a very long time. This is reason enough to devote your most careful attention to producing this infinitely delicate treat for the sensitive palate.

Start with a live lobster to ensure that the flesh will be firm and the flavor superior.

The preparation of lobster bisque requires careful attention. It must be subtly seasoned, not excessively, but with finesse. Your signature on this demanding culinary work of art will surely earn you a super cordon bleu, the coveted distinction reserved for the very highest cuisine of France.

Fish Stock

1. *Clean, peel and chop the carrots, leek, garlic and one onion. Stud the whole onion with cloves. Brown the vegetables in a saucepan with a little oil. Add the cleaned bones, then the whole onion and bouquet garni, and cook tightly covered over low heat.*

Ingredients:
2 carrots
1 leek
2 cloves of garlic
2 onions
whole cloves
3½ tbsp/50 ml oil
bones from 2 fish
1 bouquet garni
¾ cup/200 ml white wine
salt and pepper

Preparation time: 10 minutes
Cooking time: 30 minutes
Difficulty: ★

2. *Add the white wine and enough water to cover the contents of the pan. Season with salt and pepper and let simmer for 30 minutes or so over low heat.*

This fish stock is a seasoned, concentrated court-bouillon made using fish bones and trimmings. It will enable you to flavor and enhance other stocks and sauces, which are important for giving the final touch to many fish recipes.
If strained through a fine sieve and stored in a tightly sealed container, this stock will keep for several days in the refrigerator.
One of the least demanding aspects of this recipe is that it can be made from the bones of any kind of fish.
If the stock is allowed to reduce even further than instructed here, you will obtain a fairly thick liquid, a demi-glace, which is closer to a glaze and can be served in place of a sauce.
Finally, be sure to clean the fish heads and bones very thoroughly before using them to create the stock.

3. *Once the stock is done, strain it through a fine sieve. It is now ready to be used.*

Vegetable Flan

1. *Halve the zucchini lengthwise. Scoop out the flesh and cut in pieces. Cook in a saucepan with salted water. Peel and slice the carrots, then cook in salted boiling water. When tender, drain and refresh the vegetables, then purée them separately.*

Ingredients:
2 zucchini
4 carrots
4 eggs
1⅔ cups/400 ml milk
butter
salt and pepper

Preparation time: 15 minutes
Cooking time: 35 minutes
Difficulty: ✭

2. *Add 2 eggs to each purée and whisk to combine. Pour ½ of the milk into each purée. Season with salt and pepper, and mix.*

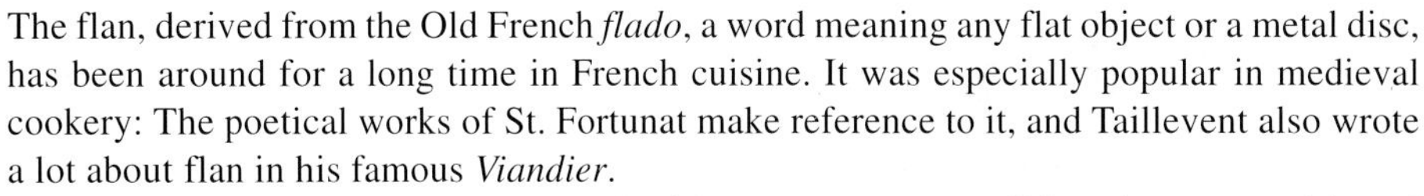

The flan, derived from the Old French *flado*, a word meaning any flat object or a metal disc, has been around for a long time in French cuisine. It was especially popular in medieval cookery: The poetical works of St. Fortunat make reference to it, and Taillevent also wrote a lot about flan in his famous *Viandier*.
In this case flan is not a sort of tart shell with a savory or sweet filling, but a vegetable and custard composition entirely independent of a crust.
The vegetables listed here are only one of a myriad of possibly variations. Any vegetables you choose should be finely chopped to yield a smooth mixture. When adding the eggs to the vegetables, whisk vigorously so they do not have time to cook.
The flan mixture can be strained through a sieve before it is cooked or, alternatively, you can leave it unstrained if you prefer a crunchier texture.
The flans should be left to cool before serving. Remove them from the ramekins when they are just luke-warm by gently sliding a knife around their edges.

3. *Butter individual ramekins. Pour the flan mixtures into the forms and cook them in a double-boiler over medium heat for 20 minutes. Remove the flans from the ramekins when just luke-warm.*

Fish Mousse

1. *Cut the chilled fish fillet(s) into chunks and purée.*

Ingredients:
1 lb/500 g fish fillet
3 egg whites
¾ cup/200 ml heavy cream
salt and pepper

Preparation time: 30 minutes
Cooking time: 30 minutes
Difficulty: ✯ ✯

2. *Add the egg whites to the fish, season with salt and pepper, and blend thoroughly.*

Hot or cold, as a main dish or accompaniment, this is a recipe that has more than one trick up its sleeve. This quick and easy mousse can be prepared with all sorts of fish, both freshwater and saltwater.

Our chef has these words of advice: The fish used to make the mousse and the mold into which it will be turned should always be well-chilled. Brush the mold with melted butter to avoid any trouble when turning out the mousse onto a serving platter.

Served hot, this mousse forms an excellent accompaniment to shrimps, mussels, oysters, prawns, mushrooms... The options are endless. Served as a cold dish with salad (tomatoes, avocados, hard-boiled eggs, anchovies...), our chef suggests accompanying it with a mayonnaise sauce flavored with tomato concentrate and a touch of Cognac.

This recipe lends itself to experimentation and can be varied almost infinitely with the addition of various combinations of herbs and fish. Enjoy!

3. *Add the well-chilled cream and blend the mixture once more until it is very smooth. Use the fish mousse following our suggestions, or if you wish, bake it in a terrine and serve it accompanied by melted butter.*

Béarnaise Sauce

Ingredients:
1 cup/250 g butter
2 shallots
1 sprig of tarragon
1 bunch of parsley
6½ tbsp/100 ml white wine
3½ tbsp/50 ml vinegar
3 egg yolks
salt and pepper

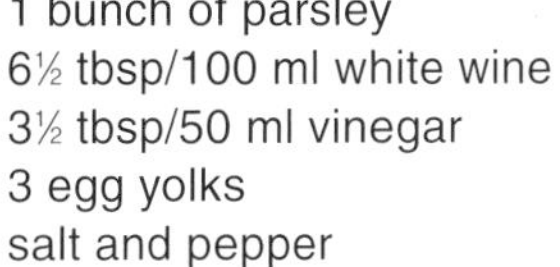

1. Cut the butter in pieces and clarify it over extremely low heat. Peel and mince the shallots; chop the tarragon and parsley as well. Place the shallots and tarragon in a saucepan. Pour in the white wine and vinegar, and reduce until the liquid has almost evaporated.

Preparation time: 30 minutes
Cooking time: 10 minutes
Difficulty: ☆ ☆ ☆

Béarnaise is a classic among French sauces, served with meat, eggs and of course fish. One of the secrets to a successful béarnaise sauce is to use a saucepan with a thick bottom that will evenly transfar the gentle heat to the contents of the pan.
When you have combined the herbs, shallots, wine and vinegar in the saucepan, bring them to a boil over medium heat and then reduce the mixture gradually until there is only a thin layer of liquid in the bottom of the saucepan.
Reduce the heat before whisking in the egg yolks. Beat the sauce without a pause; the sauce should slowly take on a thick consistency like that of mayonnaise.
Ideally, the béarnaise sauce should be transferred to a sauceboat when it is ready and served immediately. If it must wait, however, it can be kept briefly in a double boiler over hot, but not boiling, water.

2. Add the egg yolks to the reduced shallot and tarragon mixture, which should be lukewarm. Whisk vigorously so that the egg yolks do not cook. Continue to whisk over very low heat to incorporate the yolks very thoroughly.

3. Gradually add the clarified butter while whisking constantly. Make sure you do not add the whey. When ready, adjust the seasoning and mix in the chopped parsley. The sauce can be strained through a fine sieve to make it especially smooth.

Mayonnaise

1. Place the mustard in a bowl and place the yolks on the mustard. Combine and add a little vinegar.

Ingredients:
3 tbsp mustard
2 egg yolks
¼ cup/60 ml vinegar
2 cups/500 ml peanut oil
salt

Preparation time: 5 minutes
Difficulty: ☆ ☆

2. Add the oil gradually while whisking the mayonnaise vigorously and continuously.

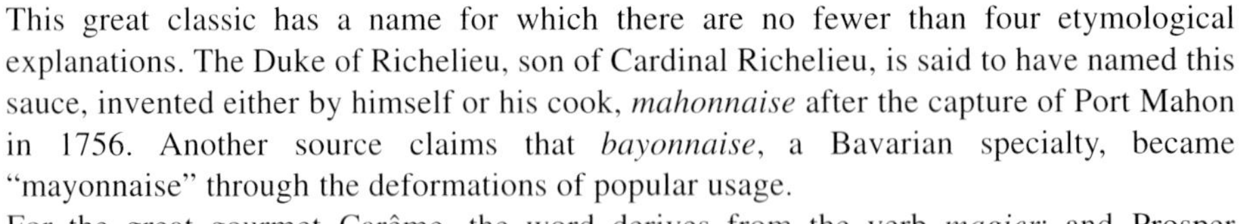

This great classic has a name for which there are no fewer than four etymological explanations. The Duke of Richelieu, son of Cardinal Richelieu, is said to have named this sauce, invented either by himself or his cook, *mahonnaise* after the capture of Port Mahon in 1756. Another source claims that *bayonnaise*, a Bavarian specialty, became "mayonnaise" through the deformations of popular usage.

For the great gourmet Carême, the word derives from the verb *magier*; and Prosper Montagné believed that the very old French word *moyeu*, meaning egg yolk, became distorted to "mayonnaise". After all, mayonnaise is simply that: an emulsion of egg yolk and oil.

Here is some advice to make a successful mayonnaise: All the ingredients should be at room temperature when you begin, so remove the eggs from the refrigerator an hour beforehand. Lemon juice or vinegar lighten up the occasionally oily flavor of mayonnaise.

This sauce does not benefit from being cold, so do not keep it in the refrigerator. Uniquely mellow and velvety, as appetising as you could wish, this mayonnaise will accompany meats, fish, shellfish or cold vegetables with lots of brio.

3. Once the mayonnaise is fluffy, add a little salt. Mix again. The mayonnaise is ready.

Nantua Sauce

1. Gut the crayfish, then wash and dry thoroughly. Brown them in a pan with very hot oil. Peel the carrots, garlic and shallots, and cut into small pieces. Add to the crayfish along with the bouquet garni and brown well.

Ingredients:
1 lb/500 g crayfish (or the shells and heads)
⅓ cup/80 ml oil
3 carrots
3 cloves garlic
3 shallots
1 bouquet garni
3½ tbsp/50 ml Cognac
1 tbsp tomato paste
1 cup/250 ml white wine
⅔ cup/150 ml heavy cream
1 tbsp flour
1 tbsp butter
salt and pepper

Preparation time: 20 minutes
Cooking time: 30 minutes
Difficulty: ☆

Nantua sauce is generally made from the shells and heads of crayfish. If you follow the chef's instructions, you will see that it is very easy to prepare.
If you use whole crayfish instead of just shells and heads, as pictured here, reserve the tails to make another recipe, for example a crayfish gratin.
This sauce can be served separately in a gravy boat as an accompaniment to quenelles, fish mousse or plain fish.

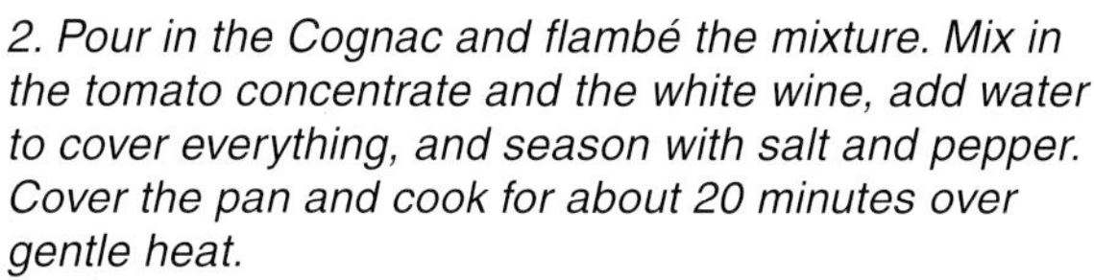

2. Pour in the Cognac and flambé the mixture. Mix in the tomato concentrate and the white wine, add water to cover everything, and season with salt and pepper. Cover the pan and cook for about 20 minutes over gentle heat.

3. Drain the crayfish and set aside. Strain the sauce through a fine sieve. Mix in the cream and let thicken for 5 minutes over low heat. Make a paste out of the butter and flour and bind the sauce with this beurre manié. Adjust the seasoning if necessary.

Glossary

Aïoli: A thick and intensely garlic-flavored mayonnaise popular in the Provence region, especially to accompany poached or boiled fish or egg dishes.

Bain-marie: A gentle method of heating used to either cook food or keep cooked food warm, a bain-marie consists of a pan containing food placed inside a larger pan of warm (but not boiling) water, surrounding the smaller pan with gently heat. Placed in an oven, a bain-marie generates steam for foods that require moist heat.

Banyuls: A sweet fortified wine made in a place in southwestern France of the same name. Port would be an acceptable substitute if Banyuls is not available.

Béchamel sauce: A basic white sauce made by adding milk to a roux. The consistency of the sauce varies greatly depending on the proportions of butter, flour and milk used.

***Beurre manié*:** A paste consisting of softened butter and flour, usually in equal amounts, used to thicken sauces or soups. *Beurre manié* and roux are both thickening mixtures of butter and flour, but a roux is cooked beforehand and *beurre manié* is not.

To Bind: Adding any of a number of substances, including flour, cornstarch, eggs, egg yolk, gelatin or cream, to a hot liquid in order to make it creamier.

To Blanch: Briefly immersing fruits, vegetables or variety meats in boiling water and then in cold water to stop the cooking. This process makes it easier to remove peels and skins, rids food of impurities, and preserves the flavor and color of food before freezing.

Bouquet garni: A combination of herbs either tied together or bound in cheesecloth and used to flavor soups, stews, etc., then removed before serving. The classic combination of herbs is thyme, bay leaf and parsley, though myriad variations exist.

To Brown: To sauté a food in hot butter or oil over fairly high heat, giving a browned exterior while the interior remains tender.

Clarified butter: Butter that has been melted slowly without stirring, then skimmed and decanted, leaving the milk solids and water in the pan. This liquid is pure butter fat and has a higher smoking point than whole butter, but less intense flavor.

To Clarify: To remove any particles which interfere with the clear appearance of liquids (i.e. jelly or consommé), usually by straining or binding the impurities, often by adding and then straining out egg white.

Court-bouillon: A flavorful broth made with clove-studded onion, celery, carrots, a bouquet garni, and occasionally lemon and garlic. Court-bouillon is most often used to boil different fish and meats.

Crème fraîche: A thickened cream with an incomparably smooth texture and nutty, not sour, taste. It is indispensable in French cuisine, particularly in sauces since it does not separate when boiled. If not readily available, crème fraîche can be simulated by adding 1tsp-1tbsp buttermilk to 1 cup heavy cream and letting the mixture stand at room temperature 8-24 hours until thickened. This will keep up to 10 days in the refrigerator.

To Defat or degrease: To skim or pour off the fat that results from cooking meat or soups, for example. This is often done before deglazing a cooking pan to make the sauce much lighter.

To Deglaze: Using a liquid such as water, alcohol or stock to dissolve food particles after food has been roasted or sautéed in it. This liquid is normally used as the basis of a sauce.

To Dice: To cut fruit or vegetables into regular, dice-like shapes. Traditional dice is between ¼ and ½ in/5 mm in size.

Double boiler: A double boiler consists of two pans that nestle into each other. The bottom pan is filled with simmering water and the top pan rests over, but not in, the hot water, providing gentle heat to melt or cook delicate foods like custards or sauces. See also bain-marie.

Duxelles: A preparation of mushrooms sautéed with shallots, butter and herbs until the liquid has evaporated. It is used as a garnish or to flavor fillings or sauces.

Emulsion: A combination of difficult-to-combine elements such as water and oil, achieved by adding the second ingredient a drop at a time while whipping continuously.

To Enrich a sauce: The finishing touch for many French sauces, this involves thickening and refining a sauce just before it is served by adding small pieces of very cold butter, or occasionally crème fraîche or egg yolk. This should be done off the heat, preferably by swirling the saucepan, but a whisk or wooden spoon may be used.

Fatback: Fat from the back of a pig, used in its natural form, rather than salted or smoked. Compare to salt pork.

Fillet: Any boneless piece of meat or fish.

Filleting fish: To separate the flesh of a fish from its bones to obtain fish fillets.

To Flambé: To pour alcohol over food and light the alcohol, imparting a very special flavor. This can be a dramatic presentation or an earlier step in the cooking process

Galette: Traditionally a flat, round pastry or any kind of tart.

To Garnish: Decorating a dish to make it more visually appealing with various edible elements; also refers to the decoration itself. Garnish varies from a single piece of parsley to the additions to a soup to entire dishes served with the main entrée.

Hot oven: 400–425 °F or 205–220 °C

To Julienne: To slice foods, primarily vegetables, into thin, regular matchsticks; also refers to foods sliced in this way.

To Knead: To thoroughly combine and work the components of a dough either by hand or with the dough hook of an electric mixer to produce a homogenous dough. It can take 15 minutes or longer to produce a smooth, elastic dough when kneading by hand.

Langoustine: Commonly, but inaccurately, called prawn, these crustaceans resemble tiny Maine lobster and are not to be confused with shrimp.

To Line: To cover the inside of a mold or pan with whatever ingredient is called for. For a charlotte, lady fingers would be used. For aspic, the mold would be lined with gelatin.

Low oven: 300–325 °F or 150–165 °C

To Marinate: To soak meat, fish or other foods in a marinade (aromatic liquid) for a period of time to allow the meat or fish to develop a deeper, richer flavor and become more tender.

Melon baller: A special spoon shaped like a tiny bowl used to carve circles from melons and other fruits and vegetables.

Mirepoix: Diced combination of vegetables, usually including carrots, onions and celery, which are browned in butter and used to add flavor to stews, sauces, etc.

Moderate or medium oven: 350–375 °F or 175–190 °C

Mousseline: Describes foods to which whipped cream or beaten egg whites have been added in order to lighten them, or simply food (usually puréed) with a light, airy texture.

To Nap: To cover food with a thin layer of its accompanying sauce.

Pineau: A sweet, white fortified wine made in the Cognac region of France. If this is unavailable, a mixture of grape juice and cognac may be substituted.

To Poach: A method of cooking food by immersing it in hot, but not boiling, water or other liquid.

To Reduce: The fundamental step in sauce preparation is to cook a mixture until much of the liquid has evaporated, resulting in a thicker and more intensely-flavored sauce.

To Refresh: A means of preventing foods from continuing to cook in their own heat either by immersing the cooking pan in ice-cold water or running cold water directly onto the food.

To Roast: A slow method of cooking food uncovered in the oven, which allows tender meat or fish to brown and caramelize on the outside, while remaining moist and tender on the inside.

Roux: A combination of flour and butter used to thicken sauces. Unlike beurre manié, roux is cooked for several minutes before any liquid is added, and has different levels of readiness: light, medium and dark.

Sabayon: Also known by its Italian name, zabaglione, this extremely light and frothy custard consists of egg yolks, wine and sugar whisked together over the gentlest of heat, usually in the top of a double boiler.

Salicornia: An edible plant that grows in shallow waters along Northern American coasts, fresh salicornia is available from summer into fall.

Salt pork: Fat from the belly and sides of a pig that is cured with salt. It is often blanched to reduce its saltiness. Compare to fatback.

To Sauté: A method of cooking in a very small amount of hot oil or other fat, usually in an uncovered pan. Food may be lightly sautéed (see to brown), or cooked all the way through.

To Scallop: To thinly slice meat, fish or crustaceans. The sliced portions are also referred to as scallops.

To Sear or seal: To brown food very quickly, usually by sautéing it in pre-heated fat, so that its surface seals or locks in the food's natural juices.

To Skim: To remove any impurities (fat, foam, etc.) which form on the surface of a liquid, particularly soups or stocks.

To Stew: To cook by simmering food just covered in liquid for a prolonged length of time. Stew also refers to the resulting dish, which is usually savory, but can also consist of fruit.

To Strain: To pour or press ingredients through a sieve or alternatively through a piece of cheesecloth in order to remove impurities, lumps, or seeds.

To Sweat: A method of cooking vegetables, especially onions, or other ingredients over low heat in butter or oil until they are transparent, without letting them brown.

Tournedo: A very lean cut of beef tenderloin, just 1 in/2.5 cm thick, or a thin and similarly succulent cut of other meat or fish.

Truffle juice: The liquid won during the process of drying the celebrated truffles. An excellent and less costly means of adding the flavor of truffles, it is available from gourmet shops. Truffle oil, high quality oil in which truffles have been steeped, is another alternative.

Very hot oven: 450–475 °F or 230–245 °C

The Participating Chefs

Lionel Accolas
Chef de Cuisine
Chevalier du Mérite Agricole

Nicolas Albano
Maître Cuisinier de France

Marc Bayon
Maître Cuisinier de France
Membre de l'Académie Culinaire de France
Finaliste des Meilleures Ouvriers de France

Marcel Benoit
Chef de Cuisine

Michel Bignon

Jean-Pierre Billoux

Luce Bodinaud

Jean-Claude Bon
Maître Cuisinier de France

Jean Bordier
Meilleur Ouvrier de France 1979
Maître Cuisinier de France
Membre de l'Académie Culinaire de France

Jean-Paul Borgeot

Dominique Bouchet
Membre de l'Académie Culinaire de France

Hubert Boudey

Maurice Brazier
Chef des Cuisines
Maître Cuisinier de France
Membre de l'Académie Culinaire de France
Officier du Mérite Agricole

Jacques Cagna
Maître Cuisinier de France
Officier du Mérite Agricole

Jacques Chibois
Chef des Cuisines

Marc Daniel
Chef de Cuisine

Alain Darc

Francis Delage
Grande Poêle d'Or 1977
Chevalier de l'Ordre national du Mérite

Joseph Delphin
Maître Cuisinier de France
Membre de l'Académie Culinaire de France

Francis Dulucq
Maître Cuisinier de France
Membre de l'Académie Culinaire de France

Sylvain Duparc
Chef des Cuisines

Maurice Dupuy

Robert Dupuy
Membre de l'Académie de France

Roland Durand
Meilleur Ouvrier de France
Maître Cuisinier de France

Gilles Étéocle
Maître Cuisinier de France
Meilleur Ouvrier de France 1982

Jean-François Ferrié

Charles Floccia

Denis Franc

Roland Gauthier

Pierre-Jean et Jany Gleize
Maîtres Cuisiniers de France

Charles et Philippe Godard
Maîtres Cuisiniers de France

Lionel Goyard
Chef de Cuisine

Bernard Hémery

Jean-Pierre Lallement
Maître Cuisinier de France

Serge de La Rochelle

Jean-Michel Lebon

Jean Lenoir
Maître Cuisinier de France
Finaliste Meilleur Ouvrier de France 1954–1961

Bernard Mariller
Chef de Cuisine

Paul-Louis et Michel Meissonnier
Maîtres Cuisiniers de France

Christian Métreau
Chef de Cuisine

Jacques Muller
Maître Cuisinier de France

Daniel Nachon
Chevalier de l'Ordre du Mérite

Jean-Louis Niqueux
Chef de Cuisine

Alain Nonnet
Chef de Cuisine
Maître Cuisinier de France
Finaliste Meilleur Ouvrier de France 1976

Angelo Orilieri
Membre de l'Académie Culinaire de France
Chevalier du Mérite Agricole

Claude Patry
Chef de Cuisine

Christian Ravinel
Chef de Cuisine

Claude Ribardière

Roger Roucou
Président des Maîtres Cuisiniers de France

Georges-Victor Schmitt
Chevalier du Mérite Agricole

Pierre Sébilleau
Chef de Cuisine

Dominique Toulousy
Maître Cuisinier de France

Gilles Tournadre

Jean Truillot
Chef de Cuisine

Jean Vettard
Maître Cuisinier de France

Pascal Vilaseca
Chef de Cuisine
Premier Mondial du Grand Prix

Index of Recipes

BASIC RECIPES